TWAYNE'S WORLD AUTHORS SERIES

A Survey of the World's Literature

Sylvia E. Bowman, Indiana University

GENERAL EDITOR

POLAND

Adam Gillon, State University of New York
College at New Paltz

EDITOR

Adam Mickiewicz

(TWAS 6)

TWAYNE'S WORLD AUTHORS SERIES (TWAS)

The purpose of TWAS is to survey the major writers —novelists, dramatists, historians, poets, philosophers, and critics—of the nations of the world. Among the national literatures covered are those of Australia, Canada, China, Eastern Europe, France, Germany, Greece, India, Italy, Japan, Latin America, New Zealand, Poland, Russia, Scandinavia, Spain, and the African nations, as well as Hebrew, Yiddish, and Latin Classical literatures. This survey is complemented by Twayne's United States Authors Series and English Authors Series.

The intent of each volume in these series is to present a critical-analytical study of the works of the writer; to include biographical and historical material that may be necessary for understanding, appreciation, and critical appraisal of the writer; and to present all material in clear, concise English—but not to vitiate the scholarly content of the work by doing so.

Adam Mickiewicz

By David Welsh

University of Michigan

Twayne Publishers, Inc.   ::   New York

to R. G. M.
. . . obiit . . . natus est.

Preface

This study of Adam Mickiewicz is concerned with the nature of his creative imagination as expressed in his poetry, and only with his biography or his philosophical and religious ideas when these affect his work.

That the poetry is quoted in translation, or paraphrase, has an essential bearing on this study. A poem and the language it is written in are indivisible. Translated, a poem either becomes a different poem or ceases to be a poem at all. However conscientious a paraphrase may be, it bears little relation to the experience of reading what the poet himself said. Nor can the import of a poem be stated (even in the original language) since it was to articulate this "import" that the poem was created. Yet such is the power of Mickiewicz' poetry that something of his genius still shows through the fabric of a translation or paraphrase.

I have used a number of analogies to the work of other great poets of European and Russian literature in this study because I believe that Mickiewicz' poetry will acquire an extra dimension if it can be shown to rank with, and sometimes to excel great poetry in other languages. But the finest effects of Mickiewicz' work cannot ultimately be explained in terms of other writers, and this I do not attempt.

This study does not aim to render any presumptuous final judgments, nor to deliver a "certificate of genius"; rather it attempts some interpretations of the poetry as art and as the expression of Mickiewicz' humanity.

The definitive study of Mickiewicz' poetry in English is Wiktor Weintraub, *The Poetry of Adam Mickiewicz* (The Hague, 1954), to which the reader is referred for topics I have not felt justified in treating again.

University of Michigan
Ann Arbor

David J. Welsh

Contents

Contents

Chronology

1798   Adam Mickiewicz born December 24, at Nowogrodek, Lithuania.

1822   Publication of *Poems of Adam Mickiewicz Volume I* (Wilno).

1824   Mickiewicz exiled to Russia for political reasons.

1826   Publication of Mickiewicz' *Sonnets* (Moscow).

1828   *Konrad Wallenrod* published.

1829   Mickiewicz left Russia for Dresden; then moved to Paris and, later, Rome.

1832   Publication of *Forefathers' Eve*, Part III, (Paris).

1834   *Pan Tadeusz*

1840   Mickiewicz appointed Professor of Slavonic Languages and Literatures at the College de France, Paris.

1855   Mickiewicz died in Constantinople, November 26.

Chronology

CHAPTER 1

Romanticism and Balladry

THE Romantic movement in European literature was largely a revolution directed against the eighteenth-century writers' preoccupation with order and reason. Romantic poets all over Europe came increasingly to feel that there were vital and mysterious elements in the human personality which their predecessors in literature had preferred to ignore.

All new literary and cultural movements are a reaction against the principles and values of the preceding generation, but the forms taken by this reaction vary from one individual to another. For this reason, the Romantic movement had such various manifestations that it is impossible to reduce the movement to a formula. Polish Romanticism had features in common with European Romanticism, but it also had individual features, as this study of Adam Mickiewicz' poetry seeks to show.

I *"Ode to Youth"*

The Romantic revolution in literature was well under way in England and Germany by the 1790's, but it did not find its way into Poland for some three decades. The leading figure in the emergence of this new kind of poetry in Poland was Adam Mickiewicz, who was born on Christmas Eve, 1798, near Wilno, the ancient Polish city and capital of the Duchy of Lithuania. Mickiewicz was brought up and educated in this still isolated rural district of Eastern Poland. He never visited Warsaw or Cracow; and after he left Lithuania for exile in Russia in 1824, he never returned to his homeland.

Yet Mickiewicz' childhood and youth in Lithuania were to color the rest of his life and his work. These formative years provided him with a constant imaginative stimulus and with much of the life experience from which his poetry was created.

Since all his poetry grew out of or refers back to his native Lithuania, Mickiewicz is a regional poet in the fullest meaning of
that phrase. His poetry confirms the truism that poets whose
work is most closely associated with specific places or regions
are at the same time the most national and, indeed, the most universal writers.

Mickiewicz' father, an impoverished attorney, belonged to the
Polish gentry who had been settled in Lithuania since the seventeenth century. The region was united with Poland in 1386; but
three years before the birth of Adam Mickiewicz, the entire Polish state fell victim to more powerful monarchies and was partitioned between Prussia, Austria, and Russia. Each of the three
zones had its own frontiers dividing it from the others; each had
its own administrative apparatus, police, and censorship controlled from Berlin, Vienna, and St. Petersburg, respectively.
Wilno was occupied by the Russian army in 1792, and in 1795
Lithuania became a province of the Russian empire. These historical events were largely responsible for the tardy development
of Romanticism in Poland.

Mickiewicz attended the University of Wilno from 1815 to
1819. This was one of the largest and wealthiest universities in
the Russian empire; but many of the students, being Polish, knew
no Russian. During the years when Mickiewicz attended, the
university was a stronghold of eighteenth-century classicism, and
his education provided him with a thorough grounding in classical philology, poetics, and rhetoric. Mickiewicz also read widely
in Polish literature and in the writers of the Age of Enlightenment such as Voltaire. He was, in fact, brought up to respect the
literary and philosophical values of eighteenth-century classicism,
with its view of man as a civilized being living in a well-ordered,
rational society. His earliest poetry includes translations from
classical authors he admired, and imitations of the Polish poets
of the Augustan era (1765-1796).

Because of this literary background Mickiewicz' first serious
and original poem had the tone and content of an eighteenth-
century philosophical poem. Most Romantics, after all, began
their careers by writing in one or another of the genres favored
by their eminent predecessors; and Mickiewicz chose a highly
respected genre for his "Ode to Youth" (1820). To the classical

poets of eighteenth-century Europe and Russia, the ode was a representative lyrical form, which owed its high status in the hierarchy of literary genres to a close association with the Classical poets of antiquity from Pindar to Horace. The prestige of the ode as a literary genre reached its height in European poetry immediately after the French Revolution. Writers like Schiller and Hölderlin in Germany adopted the form to express their political views and the intoxication of revolutionary hopes. The French Revolution was, after all, the crucial event of the eighteenth century; no one, and least of all Romantic poets, could remain indifferent to it. Hence the ode was used to express all kinds of enthusiastic or visionary outbursts addressed to Freedom, Joy, or Mankind. Technically speaking, the ode—with its irregular metrical pattern—suited a generation of poets who felt they had exhausted the possibilities of the classical couplet perfected by their immediate predecessors.

Mickiewicz caught the visionary, often oracular tone of the revolutionary odes, with their frequent exclamations and commanding imperatives:

> Youth, give me wings!
> Let me fly above the dead world
> Into the heavenly regions of illusion!
>
> . . . .
>
> Youth, fly above the commonplace,
> And, with an eye like the sun,
> Penetrate from end to end
> The immensity of mankind!
>
> . . . .
>
> Look down! Yonder eternal mist darkens
> A region of sloth absorbed in chaos—
> It is the earth!

The dramatic effect of "Ode to Youth" is heightened by Mickiewicz' ingenuity and art in organizing the poem's metrical pattern. He accustoms our ear to a pattern formed by lines of eight or eleven syllables and then unexpectedly extends the pattern by a line of thirteen syllables or decreases the line to five or even three syllables. This varying metrical pattern, characteristic of classical odes, is intended to demonstrate by its deliberate irregularity that the poet is carried away by the force of his inspiration; it causes him to break out of the bonds imposed by meter.

"Ode to Youth" celebrates the powers of the imagination and can be read as an embryonic statement of Mickiewicz' lifelong rebellion against any kind of tyranny or despotism. In addition, the ode bears witness to his profound and unshakeable faith in the regenerating powers of poetry itself. The revolutionary implications of the poem did not escape the watchful Russian censors, who refused Mickiewicz permission to include the poem in his first published book (1822).

The "Ode" also looks back to certain philosophical ideas current during the Age of Enlightenment. Mickiewicz echoes Rousseau's Utopian longings for perfection in man, and the belief of other French philosophers, such as Diderot and Helvetius, that man possesses the ability to modify Nature itself by the exertion of innate moral forces. The "Ode" implies that man is naturally good despite his sloth and preoccupation with self, which, however, he can overcome by "enthusiasm." According to eighteenth-century thinkers and poets, enthusiasm was a creative force akin to what the Romantics were to call "the imagination." Mickiewicz acquired his knowledge of these ideas partly from diversified reading, partly through participation in a secret society formed by himself and fellow-students at the University of Wilno in 1817. The "Society of Philomats," as they called themselves, consisted of a group of young men interested in social matters and also in literature.

The imagery through which Mickiewicz conveys his poem's meaning is largely classical in tone. He does not hesitate to introduce personification, always a standard item of eighteenth-century poetic diction. Other images are associated with laurels, thunderbolts, nectar, the eye of the sun. The central image is that of the "chain of love," an infinite and unbroken chain of being, in which each human soul forms a link. The unifying force that holds the links together is love:

> Together, young friends!
> The aims of all are in universal happiness,
> Strong in unity, wise in inspiration . . .

> Ah! Shoulder to shoulder! Linked in a chain
> Let us encircle the earth!
> Let us aim our thoughts at one target!

The artful though inconspicuous transitions that give the "Ode" coherence are also classical. Mickiewicz effects them in various ways: by contrast (youth and age, stars above and night below), by theme (the life of egoism, the nectar of life), or by association (Youth, the young Hercules). Each stanza of the poem has its own shape and length, but the thought is carried over from one stanza to the next by these transitions.

Mickiewicz is displaying how much he had learned from his study of the eighteenth-century poets he admired, especially Stanislas Trembecki. The young Mickiewicz turned to Trembecki's poetry in the way that Byron turned with admiration to Pope. The study of Trembecki's elegant, urbane verse taught Mickiewicz, among other things, how to concentrate on his poetic subject while adding detail and amplifying the concept. His "Ode" is a self-contained poem in the characteristic manner of eighteenth-century poetry at its finest.

II *Revolutionary Poetic Manifesto*

Mickiewicz' choice of poetry as a vocation was deliberately made and tenaciously held to, as was Wordsworth's. For some years he worked as teacher in a small country town in Lithuania, but his main preoccupation was always poetry. The first fruits of this preoccupation was a small volume, no bigger than a man's fist, called *Poems of Adam Mickiewicz Volume I* (Wilno, 1822). These poems were as revolutionary a manifesto in Polish literature as the *Lyrical Ballads* of Wordsworth and Coleridge or the Preface to Keats' *Endymion*. Like his contemporaries in England (whom, however, he cannot have known), Mickiewicz was aware of the novelty of his poetry and felt the need to explain it to contemporary readers accustomed to the classical genres and conventions. He therefore provided the *Poems* with the Preface in which he discusses his choice of ballads and romances as the most suitable poetic form in which to express his revolutionary ideas of what poetry ought to be.

As Mickiewicz knew, the ballad had a long history in European literature, and he offers in his Preface a survey of the development of the genre. Significantly, he makes a clear distinction between the imitation ballads written by eighteenth-century versifiers and the genuine ones of tradition. The eighteenth-century revival of balladry was inspired by Thomas Percy's collection *Reliques of Ancient English Poetry* (London, 1763), which in turn contributed to the popularity in Germany of the *Kunstballade* practised by Bürger, Schiller, and others.[1] Before Percy's collection appeared, folk ballads and songs had not been regarded by cultivated people as poetry at all. Indeed, to persons of taste, such compositions were not even literature. Percy realised this situation; and in an attempt to make the naked simplicity of the genuine folk ballads palatable to the genteel taste of his contemporaries, he deliberately restored and polished the primitive originals. The process of restoring and polishing involved the addition of pathos and sentiment to the essentially unsentimental folk ballads. In this respect, Percy's versions were part of the epidemic of sentimentality that flooded Europe and damaged a great deal of art.

But Percy's contemporaries admired the sentiment Percy added to the originals; when they composed ballads of their own, they gave their imitations the same sentimental tone mainly by the use of "poetic diction," or, of words that draw attention to themselves. Poetic diction of this sort distinguishes the imitation ballads from the genuine. The poetic diction used by Lewis in his celebrated ballad from *The Monk* (1795) instantly betrays its artificiality:

> A warrior so bold and a virgin so bright,
> Conversed as they sat on the green;
> They gazed on each other with tender delight;
> Alonzo the brave was the name of the knight,
> And the maid was the fair Imogen.

This verse is expressed in a diction completely out of touch with the living language; it gives the ballad a tone entirely foreign to the genuine ballad, in which the narrator submerges his own personality and tells the tale in spare, often colorless words. The poetic effects of genuine folk ballads are produced in indirect, less obvious ways—by hints and suggestions, by imagery, rhythm, and refrain. The narrator's attention is concentrated on his tale and not on the effect he hopes to produce on his readers' sensibilities.

The ballad mania initiated by Percy spread rapidly from England to Germany and thence into Eastern Europe and Russia. In Poland, imitation ballads had been composed by Karpiński (died 1825) and Niemcewicz (died 1841), who translated Lewis' fustian "Alonzo the Brave" into Polish (1802). Despite their phenomenal popularity, the imitation ballads soon fell into disrepute on account of their poetic diction, which later poets despised. The Romantic poets, including Mickiewicz, turned back instead to genuine ballads for their models. They believed that the primitive simplicity of genuine ballads was valuable for its own sake, and that the more primitive people were, the more genuine their poetry. Poetry (they believed) would be closer to Truth if it avoided contact with artificial civilization, which to the Romantic poets often meant French literature and the culture of the Age of Enlightenment. Thus the German poet and philosopher Herder, whom Mickiewicz quoted in the preface to his *Poems*, saw salvation for German poetry in recovering what he called "its own authentic voice" by direct recourse to folk poetry and ballads.

Although Mickiewicz' predecessors Karpiński and Niemcewicz had imitated the sentimental *Kunstballade* in their original and translated ballads, Mickiewicz openly admitted his debt to their work and indeed declared he would never have written ballads had it not been for those of his predecessors. Yet Mickiewicz' ballads in the 1822 volume *Poems* are totally unlike those of either of the older poets. His indebtedness lies deeper than mere stylistic or thematic imitation. The fact was that Mickiewicz was trying to solve the same literary problem as they: the problem of how to write a ballad. Instead of following the eighteenth-century imitations (as Karpiński and Niemcewicz had done), Mickiewicz went back to the genuine folk songs and ballads of his native Lithuania. He solved the problem by jettisoning the poetic diction his predecessors had favored. To replace it, Mickiewicz had to create a new vocabulary for poetry; and his realization of this need is a yardstick of his stature as a poet. For a great poet is almost always one who can bring new life to a poetic vocabulary that has become artificial and inadequate, as all poetic vocabulary does in the course of time.

Like other Romantic poets, Mickiewicz came to the conclusion that the most suitable new poetic language was the natural language of simple people. Wordsworth had reached a similar conclusion, and it led him to populate his *Lyrical Ballads* (1798) with Cumberland beggars, idiot boys, old leech-gatherers, and solitary reapers.[2] Wordsworth believed that such people, being less given to suppressing their feelings than the more sophisticated, were more likely to express themselves in natural language. Mickiewicz did not go so far as Wordsworth in this respect, though the characters in his ballads and romances include village girls, farm laborers, a blind beggar, and a sacristan.

Mickiewicz' attitude toward his own language was closer to that of the German poets of Romanticism; in both countries the urge to return to the common folk as a source of linguistic inspiration was strengthened by a patriotic motive. Folk poetry was believed to be the truest source of national poetry as contrasted to cosmopolitan (French) poetry. The cult of the vernacular language was intensified in Poland in the early nineteenth century because of the political disasters of the Partitions, which threatened the very existence of Polish culture, tradition, and literature.

One of the elements of imitation balladry which Mickiewicz adopted in his ballads and romances was the supernatural. Bürger's celebrated *Kunstballade* "Lenore," with its spectral machinery, was greatly admired by many Romantic poets throughout Europe and was imitated by Sir Walter Scott and others. But Mickiewicz' feelings about ghosts, specters, vampires, and the like were not wholly serious. He was, after all, a university graduate to whom such notions were mere superstitions, though picturesque ones. But the common folk still believed in ghosts and specters, which could, therefore, be legitimately used for artistic purposes in poetry. Not until later in his career as a writer did Mickiewicz begin to explore more seriously the supernatural and its place in human life.

III *The Ballads*

The first ballad Mickiewicz wrote was called "This I Love," and he included it in the 1822 volume of poems, claiming that it was a translation of a country song. In fact, however, this ballad displays several strikingly original features.

The story is told by an unidentified narrator, who reveals his character by what he says. He declares he was formerly a sceptic who "used to laugh at devils, and did not believe in witchcraft." However, he is also romantically inclined; and although local rustics warn him that a cemetery is haunted, he finds himself there accidentally and declares "This I love. . . ." There "Scarce had I spoken than a terrible ghost/Emerged from the nearby waters;/White were its robes, its face white as snow,/A fiery wreath on its brow." Despite his alarm, the narrator has the presence of mind to address the ghost; and it in turn reveals to him that it is the ghost of a country girl condemned to haunt the grave of a young man whose love she spurned.

Instead of seeking to arouse tearful sympathy for the hapless ghost, Mickiewicz concentrates on the manner in which the incident is told. He is concerned throughout with arousing our curiosity—always the essential aim in a genuine ballad. The opening stanzas, in which the narrator draws attention to a specific landscape, indicate the method Mickiewicz will continue to use:

> Look, Maryla, where the thickets end,
>   To the right, a thick clump of rushes,
> To the left sweeps a pretty valley,
>   In front a stream and a bridge.
>
> Close by an old church, in it owls and bats,
>   Beside it, the mouldy frame of a bell-tower,
> And behind the bell-tower a raspberry plot,
>   And in the plot there are tombs.

Why does the narrator draw our attention to this spot? Already Mickiewicz has aroused the reader's curiosity. Next, he urges us to ask whether the local belief that this spot is haunted can be true? If it is, will the narrator see a ghost? Whose ghost is it?

Why is she condemned to haunt the cemetery? Mickiewicz carefully raises each of these questions in turn as a narrator unfolds the story, then proceeds to complete the pattern of the ballad by providing the answers.

Instead of the vague, unlocalized, and general setting of imitation balladry, Mickiewicz takes some pains to provide "This I Love" with a setting that is clearly visualised and held together by perspective. The thicket, valley, stream, bridge, and the church with a bell-tower are, we learn, in the vicinity of Ruty, a village in Lithuania known to the poet. Thus the details of the landscape are not merely decorative or intended to evoke an atmosphere; the poet is visualising them in his imagination and recreating the entire setting.

"This I Love" prepares the way for Mickiewicz' later ballads, in the poetic recreation of settings, in the use of the supernatural, and in narrative technique. Pride of place in *Poems, Volume I* is given to the ballad "Romanticism," to which is appended a significant epigraph from *Hamlet:* "Methinks I see . . . Where? In my mind's eye. . . ." By quoting Shakespeare, Mickiewicz proclaims his allegiance to the new and revolutionary movement of Romanticism. To eighteenth-century classicists, after all, Shakespeare had been a particularly barbarous writer. The general consensus of enlightened opinion regarded his plays as artistically incompetent because he disregarded the all-important unities of time, place, and action, and because he drew for his material on such matters as murders, ghosts, legends, and superstitions. Eighteenth-century classicists had not yet learned to interpret the plays as metaphors or symbols.

"Romanticism," then, with its epigraph, prepares us to expect an epitome of Romantic art.[3] As in "This I Love," Mickiewicz conveys the incident on which the ballad is based through a narrator speaking in the dramatic present tense:

> "Listen, foolish girl!"
> —She does not hear—
> "This is broad day! It's the village!
> There's not a soul near you.
> What is it you attempt to grasp?
> Whom are you calling, greeting?"
> —She does not hear.

The girl is seeing the ghost of her dead lover, and her fragmentary, almost incoherent utterances strikingly convey her state of mind. A crowd of country folk gather, convinced a ghost is present. Among them, however, is an old man who appeals

> "Trust my eye and glass,
> I see nothing here.
> Ghosts are the creation of tap-room chatter,
> Concocted in the smithy of stupidity,
> The girl is talking silly nonsense,
> And the crowd blasphemes against reason."

To this, the narrator modestly replies that

> Feeling and faith speak louder to me
> Than the glass and eye of a sage.
> You know dead facts unknown to the folk,
> You see the world as dust, as cold starlight,
> You ignore living truths, you do not see
> the miracle!
> Mind your heart, and look into it!

Mickiewicz expresses in these lines the belief, which he shared unknowingly with Wordsworth, that the truest and purest feelings were to be found in the hearts of humble, rustic people.

But Mickiewicz is also uttering a direct challenge to the tyranny of intellect and reason, which had prevailed throughout the Age of Enlightenment, and which had caused poets and philosophers to restrict human experience only to that which could be grasped by the reason. Voltaire had spoken for this age when he declared: "Examine, weigh, calculate and measure—but never conjecture!" Mickiewicz, through his "modest" narrator, is suggesting that there are other elements in the human personality of which the philosophers of the Age of Enlightenment were incapable of conceiving.

Supernatural features reappear in "Switez Lake," a ballad in which Mickiewicz makes use of a widespread folk legend. His narrator begins by urging us to survey the lake, which "stretches its bright bosom,/In the form of a great curve,/Blackened its shores by dense forest,/And smooth as a sheet of ice." By night (the narrator warns us), only the bravest of men dare approach the lake. Needless to say, the spot is haunted; fire and smoke are sometimes seen arising from the depths; and the clatter of fighting, shrieks of women, bells ringing, and the clash of arms are to be heard. The narrator emphasizes the eeriness of these happenings by questions: "What can it mean? Some say this, others that,/What of it, since no one has been to the depths?/Rumour courses amidst the country folk,/But which of them guesses the truth?" Having aroused our curiosity, the narrator proceeds to satisfy it—at least partly. He informs us that the Lord of the Manor determined to solve the mystery of these sounds and sights at the lake; and, after postponing yet again his revelations ("Shall I tell you what horrors were caught?/ Even if I do, no one will believe me. . . ."), we are told that a woman rose out of the waters. She now carries on the narrative by revealing that, in the distant and forgotten past, the women folk of a nearby castle had been threatened with death at the hands of Russian invaders. They had escaped by being miraculously turned into flowers; and, although this event has long been forgotten, it lives on in the legends of the country folk.

The next ballad "Naiad of Switez" is also set in this "real" geographical place; and it combines two motives from folklore: that of a human being loved by a water nymph, and that of the punishment of an unfaithful lover by eternal damnation. Once again, the story and the way in which the narrator tells it are as important as the visualized scenes or the feelings of the characters involved, which, indeed, are conveyed entirely through implication.

Mickiewicz allows us to overhear a narrator who, in turn, sees and overhears what is happening and who persuades us to share his mystification. The dramatic effect is heightened by Mickiewicz' use of the present tense; everything is happening *now*, and the narrator is commenting simultaneously. The ballad opens with the narrator's questions: "Who can he be, that handsome young lad?/And who is the girl that is with him?/On the banks of the livid waters of Switez,/They walk by the light of the moon." The youth is identified as a local hunter, but the narrator confesses he knows nothing about the girl: "Whence came she? In vain you'd try to determine,/Where does she go? No one has followed./Like a wet buttercup she emerges to the marsh,/Like a will-o'-the-wisp, she vanishes." The youth, too, questions the girl and urges her to come with him to his hut; she, however, fears he will not remain faithful to her: "The youth knelt down, seized a handful of sand,/Called on the powers of evil,/Vowed by the holy light of the moon,/But will he keep his word?" The narrator's question foreshadows the ballad's climax:

> The water storms and swells . . .
> A watery abyss opens its jaws,
> The girl and the young man both perish.
> The water continues to storm and to foam
> Still by the light of the moon
> A pair of frail shades wander past;
> It is the young man and the girl.

"Father's Return" abandons the ghosts and other supernatural beings, but it retains the characteristic structure and method of genuine balladry that Mickiewicz had learned to handle with complete confidence. In this ballad we are required to follow what is happening by grasping implications as Mickiewicz plunges into his narrative: " 'Go, children, all together,/Out of town, to the post on the hill,/Kneel there at the miraculous picture,/Piously say your prayers.' " The speaker does not reveal his or her identity, nor explain why the children are to pray, until the second stanza. She is evidently their mother and is anxious for the return of her husband. The children obey, and their prayers are answered by the appearance of their father, a merchant, in his cart.

Now the story takes a sudden and unexpected turn as "twelve robbers" surround them; as usual in ballads, we are told precisely how many there are. But before they can rob or murder their victims, the "oldest robber" steps forward, drives away the rest, and reveals to the children's father his motive for sparing them. He overheard the children's prayers and was reminded of his own wife and son: " 'Merchant, go back to town, I must to the forest;/Do you, children, betake yourselves/To the hillock and there for my soul,/Offer up sometimes a prayer.' "

For all the simplicity of manner in which this ballad is narrated, and the artless anecdote upon which it is based, "Father's

Return" succeeds vividly in creating a poetic life of its own. The total effect is gained in several ways: the ruthless exclusion by Mickiewicz of superfluous detail, the rapidity of dramatic action (which the economy of means fosters), and the deliberately plain language. Few of the words draw attention to themselves, and epithets are almost entirely absent.

As Mickiewicz declared in the preface to his 1822 volume of poems, the "romances" in the collection are distinguished from the ballads in being devoted to feelings rather than to the supernatural or to telling a tale. They are often dramatic in form (Mickiewicz adds), and their style is marked by the utmost simplicity. "Maryla's Tomb" conforms to these requirements. Five characters appear in turn; the first is a stranger, who asks a country girl to tell him who is buried in the tomb. She explains it is the tomb of Maryla, adding: "Look to your right—her lover approaches,/Look, her mother approaches,/Look to the left, her girl-friend approaches." All three express in turn their grief for the dead girl, in which the stranger joins before proceeding on his journey.

At least two of the remaining ballads are comic in intent and treat the Devil as ludicrous. "Mrs. Twardowski" retells, with the same economy of means Mickiewicz has already put to good effect in the earlier poems, the legend of Twardowski (a Polish variant of Faust) and his pact with Mephistopheles. Twardowski's seven years provided for in their contract are up; but, before Mephistopheles can carry him off, Twardowski reminds the Devil that he still has the right to set three tests. Mephistopheles carries out the first two, but balks at the third, which requires him to live a year with Mrs. Twardowski as her husband. Mickiewicz casts this incident mainly in the form of dialogue, which enables him to introduce vulgarisms and other colloquial, un-poetic words to add to the primitive effect he was aiming at.

The only ballad based on a genuine folk theme is "The Lilies," which is remarkable for the number of features of the genuine ballad Mickiewicz has been able to assimilate and modify for his own artistic purposes. The theme is that of conjugal infidelity and murder, and Mickiewicz announces it in the ballad's first lines—an abrupt opening that is itself suggestive of the ballad method:

> Unheard-of crime!
> A wife slays her husband!
> Him she buried in a thicket
> In a field by a stream.
> She sows his grave with lilies,
> As she sows, she sings:
> Flower, grow high,
> As my lord lies deep,
> As my lord lies deep,
> Do you grow high.

The narrative concentrates relentlessly, throughout the long poem (353 lines), on the figure of this guilty woman who is haunted by superstitious terror and her own conscience. Everything else in the ballad—description, comment, diction—is made subordinate to the one single effect obtained by Mickiewicz' intent focus on the woman. She is not the virtuous, lovesick, hapless heroine of sentimental balladry. As the tale proceeds without pause or transition, each incident is designed to give a deeper insight into her acute anxiety and guilt feelings.

In a delirium of terror at the crime she has committed, the lady "Runs down to the stream/Where an old beech grows,/To a hermit's little hut,/Knock knock, knock knock!" We learn, in passing, that the events occur during the remote Middle Ages; consequently, Mickiewicz does not expect us to judge the tale by the standards of probability of his day, or of our own. In the first few lines, Mickiewicz signals to us that we are to suspend disbelief.

The hermit seeks to relieve her terror; but, when the lady returns to her castle, "Her children stand at the gate,/'Mama,' they cry, 'mama!'/'What has become of our father?'" She prevaricates, and the children "Wait one evening,/Wait a second, a third,/They wait a whole week;/Finally they forget him." The lady, however, cannot forget her crime because

> Often in the hours of night
> Something knocks out in the yard,
> Something walks about the chamber,
> "Children," it calls, "It is I here,
> "It is I, children, your father."

Guests arrive at the castle; they are the husband's two brothers who have come to seek him. They too await his return, but the winter passes into spring, "While he lies in his grave,/And the flowers grow over him,/And they grow as high/As he lies deep." The two brothers court the lady in the belief that her husband has perished in the wars. Once again, she seeks advice from the old hermit, who promises her that sincere repentance will bring God's forgiveness. He also instructs the lady to tell her suitors they are to gather wreaths and place them on the church altar. She is to choose one of the wreaths and then marry the brother who made it. "Scarce has the sun risen,/The two young men hasten out./The lady amidst her maids in waiting,/Is conducted to the marriage." As she chooses the wreath, the brothers quarrel; and at this moment her husband's ghost appears in the church to claim her as his own.

The action, violence, and terror of this story are its main ingredients. Mickiewicz deliberately omits everything not strictly relevant to his main effects, including the motivation of his characters (we never learn why the lady killed her husband), their names, and what they look like. This omission of the irrelevant is, again, a feature of the genuine ballads.

Much of the story is presented through dialogue, often without the use of such stage-directions as "he said." Hence "The Lilies" gives the effect of a play, in which such indications are omitted altogether. The utterances of the characters are brief, direct, hurried, sometimes incoherent. Everyone is caught up in the headlong rush of events and in powerful emotions to which they can only give voice by hurried exclamations and shrieks: "'Ha! Ha! My husband will never know!/Oh, it's blood! Oh, it's a knife!/He's dead, he's dead!'" and

> "A nightmare pursues me,
> As soon as I close my eyes,
> Click, click, the latch flies up,
> I wake, I see, I hear
> He walks and breathes,
> He breathes and knocks,
> Ah, I see, I hear his corpse!"

Mickiewicz has abandoned elaborate meter in favor of seven and eight syllable lines that rhyme sometimes as couplets, sometimes as quatrains. The diction is deliberately unpoetic, even primitive in effect. This is language which has been stripped bare of ornament and imagery. The one simile is short, inevitable: "pale as a handkerchief," reminiscent of "red as a rose was she." The words are for the most part in prose order, with no poetic inversions. Mickiewicz has learned the dramatic value of verbal simplicity, which in turn is intensified by a great deal of forceful repetition—another feature of the genuine ballads. The lady's children, expecting their father's return "Wait one evening,/ Wait a second, a third,/ They wait a whole week. . . ." Mickiewicz is again telling us the precise number of things (as Keats did, when he wrote "with kisses four."). Words and phrases are repeated when literary elegance require some variant word or phrase, and this repetition catches exactly the primitive poetic technique of oral transmission.

In "The Lilies," Mickiewicz has discarded the "filter" which eighteenth-century poets used in order to purify their poetic diction and make it refined. Instead of refusing to admit into his poetry certain words because they were "low" and therefore unpoetic by classical standards of decorum, Mickiewicz extends his vocabulary to include colloquial, dialect, even vulgar words— providing they are the words by which he can best express his meaning.

Mickiewicz' ballads mark a sudden expansion of frontiers in Polish poetry. They open up a new poetic world in which all the elements contribute to the revolutionary effect. In his last poems, written in the late 1830's and 1840's, Mickiewicz was to make a significant return to the ballad form; but in this instance he put the ballad technique to the service of purely lyrical poetry. Later he returned to the ballad as the most expressive way of dramatizing his own poetic experience.

CHAPTER 2

Forefathers' Eve

ALTHOUGH the poets of the Romantic period were at their most expressive in lyrical poetry, nearly all of them regarded the drama as the supreme literary form. The English Romantics, from Wordsworth to Byron and Shelley, admired the Elizabethan drama and sought to emulate it. In 1821 Byron had said: "I want to make a regular English drama . . . a mental theatre." The French Romantics, too, went back to Shakespeare and chose the theater as their most effective weapon of revolt against classicism. The theory and the practice of the German Romantics were preoccupied with a belief that Classical Greek drama and Shakespeare could provide the finest models for a new, living form of drama. Yet they all failed to produce plays that lived up to their high theoretical ideals; the tragedies of Wordsworth, Shelley, Byron, of Pushkin and Lermontov, of Victor Hugo, Lessing and Kleist are, as George Steiner has said, but "imperfect monuments to an obstinate endeavor." [1]

Mickiewicz shared his contemporaries' enthusiasm for the drama. In the second volume of his *Poems* (1823), he published parts II and IV of *Forefathers' Eve*, which he called a poem but cast in dramatic form. He hoped that this work would give rise to a new kind of drama that was to be essentially Slavic; and, like the German dramatists, he looked back for his model first to the ancient Classical drama of Greece and also to Shakespeare. Mickiewicz knew that ancient Greek drama had been associated with pagan religious rites and ceremonies, and it seemed to him that by transferring this association to Slavic rites, his own drama would acquire the qualities that had made Greek tragedy so powerful. Eighteenth-century writers and critics had disliked Greek drama. They could not approve the uncontrolled forces of imagination expressed, for example, by Aeschylus, nor the unbridled passions depicted by Euripides. But these were precisely the qualities that the Romantic writers admired in their attempts to liberate poetry from the total control of the writer's conscious mind and reason.

I *Prefatory Materials*

Mickiewicz prefaced *Forefathers' Eve*, II, with "The Specter," a ballad, which serves as a prologue and sets the atmosphere of the dramatic action to follow. The ballad tells of a young man who is believed to have killed himself for love and is now condemned to haunt a cemetery on Forefathers' Eve. Mickiewicz is here reverting to the suicide theme that runs through his ballads—and indeed through all Romantic poetry and drama, as it had done ever since Werther killed himself for love of Charlotte in Goethe's celebrated novel, *The Sorrows of Young Werther* (1774). This novel played a significant part in bringing the Age of Reason to a close by rejecting the eminently rational idea that sense could triumph over sexual passion. Goethe's novel proved to the satisfaction of the Romantic writers and their readers that it could not.

The ballad is followed by a prose introduction in which Mickiewicz sets precisely the place and time of his play:

Forefathers' Eve is the name of a ceremony celebrated to this day among the common folk in many parts of Lithuania, Prussia and Courland, in memory of their ancestors. . . . This ceremony goes back for its origins to pagan times, and was once called the Feast of the Goat. . . . Nowadays, because enlightened clergy and landlords have tried to root out the custom, which is associated with superstition and often objectionable excesses, the folk celebrate Forefathers' Eve secretly, in chapels or empty houses near a cemetery. There they usually set out a feast of various dishes, drink, fruit, and conjure up the spirits of the dead. It is remarkable that the custom of offering food to the dead seems common to all pagan peoples, from ancient Greece in the times of Homer to Scandinavia and the East, and to the present in the islands of the New World.

By selecting this folklore religion with all its ghosts and demons, Mickiewicz is clearly following the contemporary trend of thought that rejected the religious world of order of the eighteenth century. But, for all the authenticity he claims for depicting the rite of Forefathers' Eve, Mickiewicz does not present it in a naturalistic manner. Instead, he uses the essentially anti-naturalist convention of the poetic drama, in which the characters speak poetry. As in the ballad "Romanticism," he quotes Shakespeare to adumbrate his theme: "There are more things in Heaven and Earth. . . . Than are dreamt of in your philosophy." Despite the erudite preface to *Forefathers' Eve*, Mickiewicz cannot have known the deeper significance of these world-wide ancestor rites, though his imagination may intuitively have discerned it. As present-day psychologists have suggested, these rites may in essence represent attempts by primitive man to lessen or abolish altogether the barriers between conscious mind and the unconscious, which is the "true source of life." [2]

II *The Evening Ritual*

Forefathers' Eve, Part II, takes place in a country church at evening. A sorcerer or wizard is discovered, accompanied by a chorus of villagers led by an old man. All utter cries of alarm as the wizard bids them

> Shut the chapel door,
> Stand around the coffin;
> No lamp, no candle,
> Hang shrouds over the windows,
> Let not the pale brightness of the moon
> Fall in here through crevices.

The wizard performs the necessary rites, then bids the villagers prepare for the apparitions he is about to conjure up by offering "alms, prayers, food and drink." The first spirits to manifest themselves in response to his summons are the Unresolved spirits of two children. They are in Limbo, where Catholic doctrine places unbaptised infants: "Although we have plenty of everything,/ Fear and anxiety torment us,/ Ah, mama, the road to Heaven/ Is closed to your children!" When the wizard asks what they need to reach Heaven, the child replies:

> We have come to Forefathers' Eve
> Not for prayers or feasting,

> We need no oblatory mass:
> We ask not for cake, milk, fritters,
> We ask for two grains of mustard.

The mustard is requested because, by God's command, he who has never known sorrow in this world cannot know joy in Heaven. The wizard grants their request and then exorcises them by the ritual: "Avaunt!"

The children's spirits are followed by an Unredeemed spirit. He is the Lord of the Manor, whose evil deeds during life have placed him in Purgatory. As he appears, the wizard describes him to the terrified villagers: "Look, Look! that countenance!/ Smoke and lightning in his mouth,/Eyes starting from his head,/ They glow like coals in ash." The apparition calls to the villagers, reminding them, "I am your late master, children!/This was my village, indeed./Scarce have three years past/Since you laid me in my grave." But he is in the power of the Evil One, and suffers terrible torments as he wanders over the earth, followed by rapacious birds. The birds themselves verify his complaint in a chorus:

> He begs in vain, he weeps in vain,
> We here in a black procession—
> Screech owls, ravens, eagle owls,
> Formerly your servants, sir,
> Whom you starved with hunger,
> We will eat the food, we will drink the drink.

Whatever the villagers offer in the way of food, the birds will seize and the spirit admits: "God's ways are justified!/For he who was never a man,/No man can help."

Next of the spirits to be conjured up is an Unanswered spirit —that of a village girl. The wizard describes her: "On her head a pretty wreath,/In her hand a green twig,/And before her runs a lamb,/And above her flies a butterfly." The girl laments that she died young and so knew neither cares nor happiness. Consequently, she is not of this world nor of the next; and she is unable to ascend to Heaven or descend to earth, for, "according to God's command,/He who never touched the earth,/He can never be in Heaven." Promising the girl she will find forgiveness in time, the wizard announces the end of the rites at cock-crow. As the villagers prepare to leave the chapel, however, they are unexpectedly confronted with another ghost, who appears without being called for and who refuses to speak when the wizard questions him. He approaches one of the village girls and gazes at her intently despite the wizard's attempts to dismiss him with cries of "Avaunt! Avaunt!" The play ends abruptly, and the audience is given no indication who the young man may be.

III *All Souls' Day*

The fourth part of *Forefathers' Eve* takes place on All Souls' Day, and this time the action is preceded by an epigraph from Jean-Paul Richter, a favorite novelist of many Romantic poets, which suggests the subjective and lyrical mood of what follows. However, the setting of the play prepares us for a drama of ordinary family life; it depicts "A Priest's house, the table laid, supper just over. . . . Two candles on the table, a lamp burning before a picture of the Blessed Virgin—a chiming clock on the wall." All of these stage properties contribute at the appropriate time to the drama; even the three lights (two candles and the lamp) are significant, partly because they will suddenly go out at important moments of the play and partly because they remind an informed audience of the old superstition that three lights in a room attract ghosts.

The Priest and his two children have just finished their supper when the curtain rises, and at once a "strangely dressed" Hermit enters. The children—wiser than the Priest in this respect—instantly recognize the Hermit as a ghost. He is, indeed; and like all ghosts, he has come to the Priest's house for a purpose. But before he reveals it, the Hermit pronounces an extended "confession." *Forefathers' Eve,* IV, consists of this confession; the entire drama takes the form, therefore, of a monologue in which the dramatic action takes place and in which the Hermit recreates events in his own past, ponders over them, and conveys to the other protagonists and to the audience the state of his own mind.

The Hermit's monologue falls into three parts, each marked by the chiming of the clock on the stage. The first part is his "hour of love," in which the Hermit dwells on the nature of his passion in agitated, even distracted terms. His agitation is emphasized by the irregular, often broken lines, which ebb and flow as he struggles to achieve coherence. Like Ophelia in her madness, the Hermit breaks off from time to time to sing snatches of old ballads that echo his suffering.

When the clock strikes ten (Mickiewicz is exploiting "stage time"), the Hermit's agitation gives way to despair and to his "hour of anguish." As the hour begins, the Hermit reveals his identity to the Priest. He is Gustav, whom the Priest knew as a child; and, from this point on, the Hermit "becomes" Gustav, although in appearance he remains the same "strangely dressed" individual. Mickiewicz does not comment on this transformation, but it foreshadows the transformation theme which was to pre-occupy Mickiewicz in *Konrad Wallenrod* (1828); in *Forefathers' Eve*, III, (1832); and in *Pan Tadeusz* (1832-34).

During the second hour, the feverishly irregular verses of the first hour of love yield to the stately rhythm of thirteen-syllabic couplets (Alexandrines), the traditional meter of Polish classical tragedy. Yet Gustav's words do not lose their undercurrent of passion. The impression these passages give is, rather, of melting sentiments held in check only by the precision of meter and language, of explosive emotion controlled only by regularity of rhythm.

Gustav recollects a visit he made to his now deserted childhood home (as Mickiewicz had done in 1821). The visit leads him, by association, to recall his idyllic childhood and his first meeting with the girl he was later to love. She is the heroine of Gustav's drama and the cause of his tragedy. Gustav recalls that "Lately I visited the home of my dead mother,/Scarce could I recognise it! Little remained!/Wherever you look—tumble-down, deserted and destruction!" Of all the household only an old dog survives, but he too dies on recognising his former master. Gustav's recollections now extend further back in time, to his childhood and youth, and to the rural landscapes where he first met his beloved: "Henceforth she was mistress of all my deeds, wishes, thoughts,/Henceforward for her alone, of her, through her, after her!" They read Rousseau together; he built her a bower, brought flowers and berries; and it was also there that

she caught "A silver-plumed carp, a trout red-mottled." The
Priest seeks to comfort Gustav with a platitude: "alas, the pain of
memory/Consumes us, yet nothing around is changed!"

Suddenly Gustav breaks off; when he returns to his recollections, he has already lost his beloved. He revisits a garden where
they used to meet: "The same firmament shaded with clouds,/
The same pale moon and glistening dew . . ." The same evening
star is shining; the same feelings burn within him: "Everything
was as it had been—but she was not there!" On leaving the garden in despair, a mysterious power draws Gustav towards the
manor where

> A thousand lights dissipate the northern gloom,
> The clatter of riders and rattle of carriages is heard.
> Now I am at the wall, stealthily I approach,
> Force my gaze through the crystal panes,
> All the tables are laid, all the doors shut:
> Music, singing—they are celebrating some occasion!

The Priest warns Gustav that he was involuntarily seeking torment. Then "the angel of death" leads Gustav from the paradise
garden; and, as he continues to recall his sufferings, his tone
grows increasingly grief-stricken. Yet under the main current of
elegiac emotion, we begin to perceive a counter-current of irony,
directed against Gustav himself and against the woman:

> Woman! Vain dross! aery being!
> The angels envy your features,
> Yet your soul is worse, worse than . . . !
> O Heavens! Gold has blinded you!
> And the gleaming bubble of fame, empty within!
> So be it! Let everything you touch turn to gold;
> Wherever you turn your heart and lips,
> You shall kiss, embrace frozen gold!
> I, if I could choose
> Even the most divine form of woman
> The like of which God has not created,
> More beautiful than angels,
> Than my dreams, than the inventions of poets,
> Even than thou thyself—I would give her for you. . . .

At the height of his despair, Gustav draws a knife; and, although the Priest seeks to prevent him, he turns its blade on himself. But time is pursuing him, and at this moment the clock strikes again, a cock crows, the second candle goes out of its own accord, and the third, final hour begins.

This is the "hour of warning," in which Gustav reveals his purpose in visiting the Priest's house. He has come on behalf of the spirits of the dead to beseech the Priest not to forbid the rites of Forefathers' Eve. When the Priest refuses to accede, Gustav reproaches him: "If the earthly covering were to fall from your eyes/You would see more than one life around you/Driving on the dead clay of this earth." Then the witching hour of midnight strikes and the cock crows. Gustav vanishes, and an impersonal chorus of voices echo his last words which in turn echo a theme of Part II: "Let us listen and attend/That, according to God's command/He who once was in Heaven while he lived/Will not gain Heaven soon."

IV *Tragic Hero*

Gustav is Mickiewicz' contribution to the self-dramatizing Tragic Hero of Romantic poetry and drama. But he is also a Tragic Hero in the Aristotelian sense since he is brought low by some error of judgment (excessive love for an object which proved unworthy). Gustav's reason has been overthrown by passion, his mind reduced to a state bordering on chaos, his personality almost destroyed by overwhelming emotions. This is the reason he can only be a ghost, and the reason the play ends with his total disintegration. Mickiewicz is suggesting that Gustav's emotions are beyond human endurance. Yet Mickiewicz also makes it clear that we are not to regard Gustav as a "person." He moves on a different plane from his environment in the Priest's homely dwelling; and so Gustav is best considered as a literary construct, possessing recognizable traits of human nature, which, however, have been simplified for dramatic purposes. He cannot be judged by the standards of actual life.

Gustav is not, however, entirely "objectivized." He expresses feelings which may well have been personal for Mickiewicz and which were not, therefore, conceived for their dramatic value alone. No doubt the particular memory of a woman Mickiewicz loved asserted itself in the play, but at the same time an idealizing process was at work in his concept of her. But we know better, nowadays, than to discuss the play by looking through it into what little we know of Mickiewicz' private life, or even to regard the play in terms of a nineteenth-century critical approach to drama as development of a "real" character on the stage. *Forefathers' Eve* is a total configuration, in which the Tragic Hero is the representation or symbol of a private wish and acts out certain of the poet's private longings. By bringing his inner conflicts into the daylight, Mickiewicz could begin to resolve them; and by calling these conflicts "Gustav," he was submitting them to the discipline of art. The function of the action is to teach the Tragic Hero the folly of his longings. By projecting his longings into the comparatively objective form of a play (with, admittedly, strongly lyrical characteristics), Mickiewicz also achieved the distance—psychological or geographical—from his material which many artists need before they can mould experience into a work of art.

Mickiewicz was reading *Hamlet* in 1822, and analogies with Shakespeare's play are unavoidable. Like Shakespeare's hero, Mickiewicz' Gustav speaks for his author and also for himself— or sometimes for one, sometimes for the other. Both Gustav and Hamlet are endowed by their authors with obstinate egoism, and both display all the suspicions of a maladjusted individual. Both seek escape from the complexities of life, and their sufferings are those of disordered minds. Both are socially isolated individuals: Gustav is a hermit, a person who has withdrawn from the world; Hamlet is set apart by his rank. Gustav is also a ghost, and therefore an elemental being, free of the obligations imposed upon man by society.

His monologue appears on the surface to be a romantic outburst of poetry celebrating the destructive power of love. Mickiewicz has Gustav dwell on the feature of sexual passion which the Romantics found especially thrilling: its irrational quality, which the human intellect is powerless to resist. The prevailing eighteenth-century attitude in poetry toward love had been that love was an art, subject to rules, and was best spoken of in a witty or ironical manner, as Ovid did in the *Ars amatoria*. The Ovidian attitude is reflected in the abundant Anacreontic verses of eighteenth-century poets addressed to their coy or flighty mistresses.

The polarity between Ovidian and Romantic standards of love gives *Forefathers' Eve*, IV, its dramatic tension. By exposing passion as destructive to man, Gustav is arguing all the time against Ovidian standards. The Priest's function (like that of Polonius in *Hamlet*) is to console Gustav by voicing a number of sensible and rational aphorisms: "Let us not lose hope, joy follows sorrow, God will take into account in the next world all your sins in this one. . . ."; "Man is not created for tears and laughter, but for the good of his neighbors." The Priest's aphorisms are not mere moralizing, however. They are true, even though they may not be very valuable as currency, and, indeed, are more often than not irrelevant to Gustav's predicament.

There is no moral meaning in the play, for Mickiewicz did not intend to provide one. Essentially the work's meaning is contained in the state of feelings it expresses in poetic form. As Gustav's monologue proceeds, Mickiewicz is exerting critical control of his material and generating poetry by all the means at his disposal—rhyme and meter, word order, figures of speech, and imagery.

V *Imagery*

Imagery lies at the heart of Mickiewicz' poetry. His imagery makes Mickiewicz a "modern" poet in contrast to earlier poets who regarded imagery as ornament. The Romantic poets, including Mickiewicz, were the first to realize that a poem can itself be a multiplicity of images, and that images are the most poetical and economic means of conveying emotion. Instead of describing emotion, the poets could transform it into imagery and, by doing so, heighten emotional intensity.

We should not examine the imagery of *Forefathers' Eve* in isolation. Images lose their validity as soon as they are isolated for inspection because their total meaning is always modified by context, tone, rhythm, and other technical factors. Yet Mickiewicz' poetry gains its potency, strength, and quality from imagery. Taken in context, for instance, Gustav's association of the woman he loves with the moon, clouds, dew, and the evening star may crudely suggest, in a paraphrase, how the poet operates his images. Gustav presents the woman as a poetic concept associated with the purity and intangibility of these chosen images. They crystallize his state of feeling; at the same time, they create an atmosphere within the poem. Moreover, they are Gustav's natural language. Later, the same images reappear in a different light when Gustav understands the woman's real nature: the images become cold, inhuman. When he denounces her as "dross" and "frozen gold," these images and their context perform all the functions previously performed by the moon, clouds, dew, and star.

To be sure, these images are not particularly striking in themselves. There is no reason why they should be. But they are the appropriate images, and as such they constitute a sort of poetic shorthand that gains its meaning from the way they function in context. That Mickiewicz could—and sometimes did—create poetry from strikingly dramatic imagery will be apparent in his later work.

VI *Artistic Unity*

Mickiewicz' two small volumes of poems (1822, 1823) created a considerable stir in Polish literary circles, especially among the conservative poets and critics in Warsaw. This stir was largely due to the novelty of his style, diction, and technique; but the reading public was also baffled by the fragmentary, even disjointed nature of *Forefathers' Eve*. Why had Mickiewicz published parts II and IV without Parts I and III? This question has still not been adequately answered, and the eccentricity of this manner of proceeding was increased when, in 1832, Mickiewicz published a Part III that apparently has as little in common with parts II and IV as they have with one another. A Part I was discovered in draft after Mickiewicz' death, though he never published it in his lifetime.

The formal disparity between the parts of the work does not imply any lack of artistic unity within the parts. The incompleteness of *Forefathers' Eve* denotes, rather, that Mickiewicz was working under the same compulsion as other Romantic poets who sought to express themselves in long, continuous works of art which ended only with despair or death. Wordsworth labored under this compulsion in *The Prelude,* so did Byron in *Childe*

Harold, Shelley in *Queen Mab* (1813), and Słowacki in *The King Spirit.*

Possibly the fragmentary nature of parts II and IV is due at least in part to the specific literary influence of Lawrence Sterne, an early exponent of the fragmentary as a form of literary composition in its own right. His *Tristram Shandy* and *Sentimental Journey* were widely read in Germany, Eastern Europe, and Russia during the early Romantic period. Indeed, Sterne was one of Mickiewicz' favorite authors during his student days in Wilno. Both Sterne's books lack conventional endings: the *Sentimental Journey* breaks off in the middle of an episode; and the chronology of *Shandy* is deliberately disordered, with whole chapters omitted and pages left un-numbered. Another example of this form of composition was the 1790 version of Goethe's *Faust,* which he called "A Fragment." Coleridge's "Kubla Khan" and Keats' *Hyperion* also come to mind in this connection.

Essentially, the publication of a work of art in fragmentary form allowed poets, novelists, and dramatists to take liberties with the rules that eighteenth-century writers preferred to observe. Instead of concerning themselves with the mechanics of drama or with the models provided by literary genres, Romantic writers were able to concentrate all their attention on whatever they wanted to express: on the content of their work, not on the form.

Another artistic form which shared this liberating quality with the fragmentary was opera. To 1770, opera had been even more artificial and rigid in form than classical tragedy. Then the composer Gluck and his librettist, the poet Metastasio, rejected the formality of their predecessors and sought to create a new art form—the music drama. In earlier opera, form had been paramount, but Gluck and Metastasio strove to blend form and content into a harmonious whole. The result, they believed, would be an art form close to Classical Greek drama.

Mickiewicz knew Metastasio's theories on the music drama, and we know from Kubacki's enlightening study that the young poet was impressed by them.[3] Certainly elements of opera and music drama can be discerned in *Forefathers' Eve* from the duets, recitatives, and airs in Part II to the dramatic quotations from Mozart's *Don Giovanni* in Part III. Attempts have been made to produce *Forefathers' Eve* on the stage in an "operatic" style with musical accompaniment. But it is a difficult play to stage in any style, and agreement has not yet been reached on the perfect way to produce this long, often enigmatic work. Mickiewicz himself called it a "poem," implying that, although it was cast in dramatic form, it was not primarily intended for stage presentation. Nevertheless, like the plays of Shakespeare, *Forefathers' Eve* seen on the stage discloses things hidden to the reader, but a reader can discover other things which no actor or stage performance will reveal.

CHAPTER 3

The Sonnets

IN October, 1823, the Russian police in Wilno arrested Mickiewicz and other members of the Philomat secret society, with whom he had maintained contact since his university years. They were suspected of anti-Russian sentiments, and Mickiewicz was imprisoned for seven months in a local monastery, which had been converted into a prison for political detainees. Then the poet and most of his companions were sentenced to exile in Russia. At first Mickiewicz lived in St. Petersburg, later in Moscow and in Odessa. He was not treated as a criminal, for he made his way into fashionable literary society in the Russian capitals where he met Pushkin and other poets and writers. However, few details are known of Mickiewicz' five-year sojourn in Russia. His doings and whereabouts for weeks, even entire months at a time, are unrecorded. Not until after two years' exile did he succeed in publishing a volume of *Sonnets* (Moscow, 1826), which caused as much enthusiasm among his own generation and as much criticism from the Warsaw classicists as had his *Poems* of 1822-23.

I *The Debt to Petrarch*

Like all great poets, Mickiewicz was constantly experimenting, but he was also well aware of his substantial debt to Polish and European literary traditions. Because of this awareness, his experiments in poetry were never merely eccentric or extravagant, though his classical critics may have thought they were. In essence, Mickiewicz' constant experimenting throughout his career as a poet was directed toward an increase in his response to enlarged experience and to more profound emotion. This heightened response could be obtained, in part, by an ever-increasing mastery of technical skill—one always controlled, however, by Mickiewicz' native genius, critical intelligence, and taste. His experiments were therefore in style, versification, diction, and content, rather than in form. Thus the ballads, though new and strikingly original in diction and content, were cast in a traditional form. In the same way, the 1826 sonnets derive from a highly traditional literary form but are experimental in treatment.

Mickiewicz had few Polish models in the sonnet form with which he could compete, and it was natural that, familiar with European poetry as young Mickiewicz was, he should turn to the Petrarchan sonnet. The sonnets of Petrarch are characterized by a rigid framework and an elaborate rhyme and metrical system, into which the poet has to fit his material. The rigidity of the sonnet's framework facilitated the orderly presentation of thoughts and feelings by Petrarch and his imitators.

Mickiewicz expressed his debt to Petrarch in the epigraph to the first cycle of twenty-three sonnets in the 1826 volume: *Quand'era in parte altr'uomo da quel ch'i'sono* ("When I used to be in part a different man from what I am"). This line comes from the sonnet Petrarch composed as a preface to his collection celebrating the beautiful Laura. The sonnet's tone is distinctly at variance with the yearning and love-sick tone of the rest of the collection. Petrarch suggests he is now looking back wryly, even ironically, at his "other self"—at the man he had been when composing the Laura sonnets. He refers in an almost sardonic manner to his "delirio d'amore," his "vain hopes and griefs" and "juvenile errors." That Mickiewicz caught this ironical note in his Italian model is suggested by the ironical undertone audible with varying degrees of clarity in his own first cycle.

As might be expected from the epigraph, the cycle treats of love. Yet, although Mickiewicz is the central figure in Polish Romanticism, the kind of love he celebrates in the cycle is not "Romantic." This love is far from the ecstatic, despairing, introspective passion to which Gustav gave utterance in *Forefathers' Eve*, IV. It is, rather, love of the Classical sort cultivated by Ovid and by his countless admirers who wrote European poetry. Throughout the cycle, Mickiewicz is concerned with *arte regendus Amor* ("Love is ruled by art"—Ovid, *Artis amatoriae liber I*). Such love is ruled by a tyrannical Cupid armed with "darts" and "barbs"; and it is marked by a strain of sensual realism that is also characteristic of the poetry of Ovid, Anacreon, and their

[44]

admirers. Mickiewicz thus enumerates his physical symptoms: "Scarce did I see you, than I was afire . . ./Scarce did you start your song, than I dropped a tear." (I) He talks to himself, contradicts himself in conversation with other people: "My heart beats violently, I cannot draw breath,/Sparks flash before my eyes, I turn pale;/More than one of those present inquires after my health." (II) He cannot tell whether it is pain or delight he feels in his love:

> When I feel the touch of your hand
> When I catch a flame from your lips,
> Dearest! Can I call that suffering?
> But when our countenances are bathed with tears,
> When the vestiges of life are borne away in sighs;
> Dearest! Can I call that delight? (V)

Mickiewicz' eighteenth-century predecessors—Karpiński, Kniaźnin and Trembecki especially—would have sympathized with the young poet; indeed, they had enumerated identical symptoms in their Anacreontic poetry of the 1770's and later.

II *Style and Tone*

Mickiewicz' beloved, like Kniaźnin's Eliza, is "cruel" (II). She appears in the attire of a shepherdess (III)—very appropriate garments for a poet's mistress taking part in a pastoral idyll. In Sonnet X, a Cupid peeps out of her bright eyes and aims his arrows at the poet. In Sonnet IV, we overhear the lovers' hurried conversation at their "rendezvous in a thicket": " 'Is it you? So late!'—'I missed my way/Among the thickets by the moon's uncertain light:/Did you yearn for me? Did you think of me?' 'My dear ungrateful one!/Ask me whether I could think of anything else?' " We are reminded of Karpiński's pastoral idyll *Laura and Filon* (1780), while the elegantly elegiac tone of the same poet's *Recollections of Past Love: A Pastoral Song* is echoed in Mickiewicz' Sonnet VIII, which depicts the poet's beloved one gazing at her reflection in the river Niemen. This memory prompts the poet to ask: "Niemen, domestic river! Where are the springs of yesteryear,/And with them so much joy, hopes so great?/Where is the pleasant cheer of infant years?/. . . Where is my Laura?"

Sonnets VII and X, adapted from Petrarch, are examples of the "blazon," or list of the beloved's qualities, a minor genre much practiced in earlier Polish poetry. Kniaźnin's *Prima Aprilis* (1779) opens with the greeting "Good day!" which Mickiewicz uses as a key phrase in Sonnet XV. Classical allusions, which constitute a prominent item of poetic diction in eighteenth-century poetry, make an appearance here and there throughout the first cycle of sonnets: Diana, the Muses, Parnassus, the Danaïdes, the poet's Alcaic lute are all included. Mickiewicz had strictly excluded these theatrical properties from his ballads, narrative poetry, and *Forefathers' Eve;* and he was to exile them from the second cycle of *Crimean Sonnets.*

The echoes, references, and allusions to the conventions of Rococo pastoral and Anacreontic poetry give the first cycle its characteristic tone. Mickiewicz heightens this tone by a variety of stylistic devices. Sometimes he will use hyperbole, as when he "rehearses in my mind words/With which I am to curse your cruelty,/Composed, forgotten, a million times." (II) The entire gathering in a ballroom falls silent as his beloved enters (III), or he fears the vestiges of life will be wafted away in sighs (V). Elsewhere he interjects a brief aside of a sardonic nature: "And although even now a pretty face allures me,/Although I still must sing and compliment you all,/Yet earlier I'd have given everything, while today—everything except my heart." (XXI) When malicious gossip causes the poet finally to fall silent: "I rend the strings and cast my silent lute/Into Lethe. As the bard is, so's his audience." (XXII)

Still elsewhere the sardonic tone is expressed by the introduction of deliberately unpoetic words, ones not at all appropriate to love sonnets:

> Scarce do I enter, exchange a few words with her alone,
> Than the doorbell rings, in rushes a footman,
> Behind him a guest . . .
> O you accursed bore! I count the minutes
> Like a criminal awaiting the hangman:
> You idly chatter of yesterday's party. (XVIII)

Puns and diminutives also contribute to the total stylistic effect of the sonnets.

The first cycle is also close to eighteenth-century taste in its social orientation. Other people are nearly always present, or else
the lovers are in hiding from inquisitive eyes: "I fear the rustling
leaves, the cry of night birds;/Ah, we must be guilty since we are
frightened." (IV) Elsewhere, "The prude condemns us, the liber-
tine mocks." (V) Others deride the poet and declare that "This
bard merely loves, torments himself and mourns,/He feels nothing else or cannot sing." (XXII)

The importance of society is illustrated in the first cycle by the
way in which most of the sonnets are cast as dramatic lyrics, addressed to the poet's mistress or to other people. We rarely hear
the poet murmuring to himself. Several of the sonnets, indeed, are
conversation pieces, examples of that highly social art which the
eighteenth century cultivated to perfection. The settings, too, are
never far from society: Mickiewicz chooses drawing rooms, a
crowded ballroom, the vicinity of his mistress' bedroom, a garden
or thicket. Even the Niemen is "domesticated," and Laura uses it
as a looking glass. The poet implies he and his beloved inhabit a
well-ordered world that is, however, free from stiff formality and
where gallantry prevails.

Mickiewicz is voicing thoughts and feelings which any cultivated eighteenth-century reader could have shared, though he
might not have approved the tone and diction. But in the second
cycle, included in the 1826 volume, Mickiewicz uses the sonnet
form to give expression to thoughts and feelings very few eighteenth-century readers would have cared to contemplate, let alone
share. The shocked and hostile criticism with which Mickiewicz'
classically minded contemporaries greeted the *Crimean Sonnets*
provides ample evidence that the poet had entered into a world
very different from that of the first cycle.

III Crimean Sonnets

In the autumn of 1825, Mickiewicz travelled for a few weeks
through the Crimea. What he saw and, more significantly, what
he experienced during the journey evoked within him an imaginative and creative response that was totally new, not only in his
poetry but even in the entire Polish poetic tradition. He acquired
new subject matter that demanded a vastly increased imaginative
range for its expression. Indeed, Mickiewicz gained the power to

express modes of experience hitherto unexplored and even unrecognized. To be sure, descriptive poetry was much practised in the eighteenth century; but the tendency of Augustan poets, whether Polish or English, was always to impose their own cultivated taste on the landscapes they were describing. In poetry of that kind, the landscapes themselves became a pretext for wit, moralizing, or philosophizing. Besides, Augustan landscapes are invariably cultivated and controlled by poetic diction of a special kind.

Landscapes are not the theme of Mickiewicz' *Crimean Sonnets*. To the poet, the Crimea with its mysterious alternations of darkness and light, peaks and abysses, storm and calm was an experience in its own right. This unknown region provided Mickiewicz with an unconstrained expanse for projecting the unconscious content of his mind.[1] The landscapes provided a mirror in which the poet could see reflected the inner drama of his own psyche, and which he sought to integrate into his conscious mind by the power of art.

The natural and indeed the only way to approach this inner drama was through symbols. The epigraph from Goethe introduces the first of these: "He who would understand the poet/ Must travel into the poet's world." The poet's world here is the psyche from which poetry emerges, to be organized, molded, and communicated with the utmost delicacy and sensitivity at his command. An even more specific declaration of this symbolism was made by Jean-Paul Richter, the Romantic novelist, with whose writings Mickiewicz was familiar: "Our measurements of the rich territory of the *Me* are far too small and narrow if we omit the immense realm of the unconscious, this real, interior Africa in every sense." Mickiewicz' Crimea corresponds in this respect to Jean-Paul's Africa.

The cycle is a construct of symbols that are not used as decoration or for effect but spring directly from the experience Mickiewicz sought to express. All Mickiewicz' symbols speak for themselves. They are the "shaft that leads to the inner parts of the mine."[2] They are vividly realized, powerfully felt and seen, strongly imagined—not obvious or predictable. Such is the nature of these symbols, however, that we cannot successfully paraphrase or isolate them from their context; nor, of course, can they be interpreted exclusively as manifestations of the poet's unconscious.

The human psyche was the vital, mysterious element in human personality that eighteenth-century writers preferred not to contemplate, but Romantic poets eagerly sought it. They believed that, if explored and mapped, this element would assure a deeper sense of life. At the same time, however, they were often aware of the danger inherent in any attempt to entrust the self to that dark and often precipitous pathway that leads down into the depths of the unconscious. The *Crimean Sonnets* are full of cryptic warnings not to look, not to leap, not to proceed in a certain direction. Read in the light of psychology, the *Crimean Sonnets* give Mickiewicz a prominent place among the poets and philosophers who, as Freud said, "discovered the unconscious." [3] What Freud and Jung did, nearly a century later, was to discover certain scientific techniques and methods by which the human unconscious and psyche could be studied.

Images of water, darkness, and descent provide one of the keys to the cycle. The Akerman steppe, where the poet's journey begins, is likened to an "expanse of dry ocean" into which the traveler "floats," suggesting that he is not following a road but is being borne irresistibly along. The carriage "plunges like a boat" into "waves of rustling meadows" and "torrents of flowers." Dusk is falling as this "night sea journey" begins. The present tense, to which Mickiewicz adheres throughout the cycle, contributes almost imperceptibly to an effect of dramatic presence; it is as though everything were happening *now*. The territory into which the traveler is setting out is without road or sign-posts. It is the remote and unknown territory of which Novalis wrote: "The mysterious way goes inwards." The traveler's only guide is the stars, while a cloud gleams in the distance where "dawn will rise."

For all its symbols, the opening sonnet—like the rest of the cycle—also presents a landscape on which the poet's eye is fixed. The imagery is hardly ever abstract, generalized, or impalpable; and in this respect it is unlike that of Mickiewicz' contemporaries, Shelley or Słowacki. Too often in Romantic poetry we feel the poet is wrapt in a sensual dream we are not intended to examine too closely or too critically. The purpose of such writing is often to prevent us, by sheer incantation and music, from asking questions. But imagery and symbol were as important to Mickiewicz as thought, and sound was as important as all three. Despite the emotion generated by the psychic content of the *Crimean Sonnets,* Mickiewicz' critical intelligence is hard at work too. Feeling, thought, sound—all combine.

The poet's heightened psychic state is revealed as he hears the storks flying, a butterfly hovering in the grass, a snake touching the vegetation with a slimy breast. His ear is also attuned to catch any dimly audible call which may come from within himself: "In such silence—so intently do I listen/I would hear a voice from Lithuania." His homeland serves the poet here for a final glance back to a secure base; it gives him courage to proceed: "Forward, no one calls!"

"Bright water" and the stillness of the Akerman steppe persist as the sea is viewed from the heights of Tarkankut ("Silence of the Sea," II). The boat in which the journey is to proceed "rocks lightly as if held by a chain." Then the sea symbolism becomes explicit:

> O sea! amidst your sportive molecules,
> There's a polyp asleep in the depths when the sky is clouded,
> But in calm will extend its long tentacles.
> O thought! in your depths is the hydra of memory,
> Which sleeps through misfortunes and storm of passion,
> But when the heart is tranquil, plunges talons into it.

In "The Boat" (III), Mickiewicz charges the boat with poetic significance; and we are reminded of Shelley's boat in *Alastor* (1816), which is driven over tumultuous seas and emblematic of the poet's own mind.[4] Both boats hold the same symbolic overtones. The stillness and the tranquillity of the Akerman steppe and the sea now give way in "The Boat" to the uproar and violence of a storm. The poet's unconscious is making itself manifest; and, as always when this happens, there is a danger that the personality itself may be overwhelmed: "The clamor increases, monsters of the deep hover more thickly. . . ." Even the verb "hover" in the sonnet's first line betrays a symbolic meaning: it is commonly used in Polish to express the way thoughts ebb and flow

apparently at random in the human mind. The elemental force of
the tempest is expressed by the rapid succession of verbs of mo-
tion, hastily noted and then left behind: "Wind! Wind! The ship
rolls, breaks from its bonds,/It plunges, dives into a foamy chaos/
. . . and flies across the firmament." Such is this force that the
poet becomes part of the storm. He utters an involuntary cry and
"I stretch forth my hands, fall to the ship's bosom,/It seems that
my bosom urges it on:/Lightness! Vitality! Wonder! I know what
it is to be a bird." The rushing wind symbolizes the increased
power of creative energy deriving from the poet's heightened
awareness of self. The boat, in turn, is his own special talent
which prevents him from being overwhelmed.

The "Storm" provides Sonnet IV with its title: "The sun sets
blood-red, with it the remains of hope,/The wind howled with
triumph and on the watery mountains/Rising in piles from the
sea's chaos,/The angel of death has set foot and entered the ship."
The vessel begins to disintegrate, and the other human beings on
board are reduced to broken, recumbent objects. The traveler is
well aware of the peril; he envies those on board "who are bereft
of strength,/Or who can pray, or have someone to take leave of."
He himself has to proceed with the terrible journey. This sonnet
depicts in a startling manner the "transitus," or crossing of the
great water when, as analytical psychology has shown, regressive
aspects of the unconscious make themselves felt in symbols of violence, terror, death, and destruction.[5]

By this time, Mickiewicz has established the atmosphere of the
cycle. The poet's journey symbolizes his quest for a deeper understanding of himself, and this inner drama of the psyche is made
accessible to his conscious mind through projection: it is mirrored
in the Crimean landscape and expressed in poetical language.

The symbolism serves, as true symbolism always must, to provide signals for finding a way into the hidden meaning of the poetry. The sudden contrasts between one sonnet and the next, or
within a sonnet itself, also reveal the magnitude of the poet's experience as well as providing a measure of structural coherence.
The first four sonnets have established, too, that the narrator—
speaking either in the first person, or through the mask of a pilgrim—is a solitary wanderer. He is an exile from the Age of
Reason who has strayed into the Waste Land. In this respect,

Mickiewicz' pilgrim is related to other literary wanderers, from the Ancient Mariner and Childe Harold to Ishmael and Ahab. We know these characters well enough today to be able to predict the motive for their behavior and their sufferings: they are all in search of an identity, and their own mind, soul, or psyche seems the most likely place to find it.

The mountains first come into sight in Sonnet V, "A View of Mountains from the Kozlov Steppe." These gaunt emblems of eternal power and immensity are inimical to man and conceal God. They evoke wonder, awe, and terror in the pilgrim, who expresses these feelings in rising incredulity and questions: "Yonder!—Did Allah erect that sea of ice as a wall?/Or did he cast thrones for angels out of frozen cloud?/Did djinns raise these walls from a quartered continent/To bar the way to a caravan of stars out of the east?" Mickiewicz explains in a note that the djinns are "evil geniuses who used to rule on earth but were exiled by angels, and now dwell at the world's end, beyond the mountain of Kaf." They are also the demons of all wild and deserted places who populate with their dangerous presence the rejected, unknown, unfathomed factors of existence within the unconscious depths of all men.

The pilgrim's questions are answered by a Mirza, a guide figure familiar in dreams, who often marks a new stage in what Jung has called "an individual's psychic biography." The Mirza is a guardian of the threshold. He has visited the summits and is thereby endowed with special knowledge which he imparts to the pilgrim: "Yonder? I have been there: winter reigns, there I have seen/The beaks of streams and mouths of rivers drinking from her nest." The mountain is Chatyrdag, and the Mirza pictures the terrifying isolation of the peak in imagery of thunder, eagles, and stars. Yet only by advancing beyond the walls of ice can the pilgrim pass into a new zone of experience.

Mickiewicz uses Sonnet V to introduce a new item of poetic diction—that offered by exotic words and phrases. They include the names of mountains (Chatyrdag) and words borrowed from Persian and Arabic (Allah, the Divas, caravan and the like). His classical contemporaries found these elements especially barbarous, but they represent only one facet of Mickiewicz' total rebellion against the worn-out diction of his predecessors. Another facet of this poetic rebellion had been the unpoetic words used in the first cycle. Like all great poets, Mickiewicz knew intuitively that he was responsible for remaking the poetic idiom of his time; that he succeeded in doing so is a measure of his achievement.

He obtained the exotic words used in his *Crimean Sonnets* from a study of Persian and Arabic poetry, mostly in French translations.[6] A vogue for these poems and other masterpieces of Near Eastern and Oriental literature, including the *Thousand and One Nights*, had developed throughout Europe toward the end of the eighteenth century. Their effect on literary taste had been as startling as the re-discovery of the Classical writers during the Renaissance. These works revealed to the European mind a literature founded on premises radically different from anything hitherto known in Western art.

Mickiewicz' knowledge of Persian and Arabic was not especially profound, but the manner in which he turned it to artistic account suggests that even an incomplete knowledge of a foreign literature can inspire a poet by revealing to him new methods of expression. Keats' absorption in the spirit of Hellenism—without knowing any Greek—is another case in point.

The new theme announced in "Bakchisarai" (VI) is concerned with the problem of what is permanent and what merely transient in human existence—one of the central themes in European poetry: "Still great, now the domain of the Girajs is deserted./On porches and vestibules where Pashas knelt,/In the council-chambers, the thrones of power and the abodes of love,/Now hops the locust, winds the serpent." Life has ebbed away; the ruins are now overgrown with vegetation; only a fountain, flowing like Time itself, continues to play. The pilgrim asks: "Where are you now—love, power, glory?/You should have survived forever, the fountain quickly flows./O shame! You have all passed by, yet the fountain remains."

Mickiewicz was to return to this profoundly important theme elsewhere in the cycle and also in the lyrics written in Switzerland at the end of his poetic career between 1839 and 1840. In the Crimea, Mickiewicz was concerned with the "ruins of Time," a theme that preoccupied Byron in Rome and that Shelley referred to in "Ozymandias."[7]

Using the structural principle of contrast, Mickiewicz presents next in the sonnet sequence "Bakchisarai by Night" (VII). The time, as throughout the cycle, is the present: the pious inhabitants are leaving the scene, the voice of a muezzin dies away into the evening, the "silver king of night betakes himself to rest beside his beloved." The poet evokes the stillness and shadows of the ruins, which have become "granite giants,/Like demons sitting in the council-chamber of Iblis,/Under a canopy of dark."

Iblis—the Despairer—is a very appropriate allusion. Like a number of other words in this sonnet—muezzin, cypresses, minarets—the word draws attention to itself and becomes an item of poetic diction. Yet, at the same time, all these words represent the landscape in its own right; and they combine to produce the feeling that all the component parts taken together acquire an added significance. Mickiewicz did not see any need to define more precisely this significance; he did not even indicate that we should seek a remoter or implied "meaning." But, by subtly indicating the unearthly qualities of the night scene, he prepares us to accept a visionary utterance when it comes in the form of a "lightning flash" that "flies across the silent wilderness of the firmament," symbolizing a flash of intuition or of creative imagination which illuminates the "night sea journey" or Dark Night of the Soul.

The next two sonnets—"Potocka's Grave" (VIII) and "Tombs of the Harem" (IX)—make a resonant statement of the theme of transience in human life. Again Mickiewicz uses items of poetic diction in the form of "emotive words" (roses, stars, a handful of earth, tears), but the words continue to have a real meaning and are not arbitrarily used as incantations to evoke a romantic emotion. In Sonnet VIII, the poet glances back once again to his "secure base": "Yonder in the North, towards Poland, crowds of stars glitter,/Why do so many of them gleam in that direction?" In IX, the Mirza, in his role of guide to the pilgrim, expatiates on the theme of transience: "O roses of Eden! At the spring of purity/You flourished under the foliage of shame,/Hidden forever from the infidel's eye."

From time to time, Mickiewicz adds footnotes to various sonnets to explain words, or to refer to his sources in books for certain historical or geographical facts. Most Romantic poets felt this need to explain their work because, as they well knew, this new poetry was often difficult for their contemporaries, who had been brought up on eighteenth-century traditions and conventions. "Potocka's Grave" is thus provided with a footnote offering information about the actual tomb: "built in Eastern style, with a round dome," believed in legend to have been erected by one of the "last Khans of the Crimea" for a Polish slave-girl he loved exceedingly. A note to the "Tombs of the Harem" informs us that "in a delightful garden, amidst slender poplars and mulberry trees, stand the white marble tombs of Khans and Sultans, their wives and families: in two nearby charnel-houses lie coffins scattered in disorder: they were at one time richly engraved, today bare planks and rags of shrouds protrude." These harmless displays of erudition are evidence of a short-lived fondness in the young poet (he was still in his twenties) for the more theatrical trappings characteristic of one aspect of Romantic poetry. But his critical intelligence evidently warned him that such material should be excluded from the poetry; he therefore banished it to footnotes. At the same time, these notes demonstrate how often the truth of experience underlies Mickiewicz' poetic truth. The sonnets are firmly based on reality.

After the elegiac, contemplative tone of sonnets VIII and IX, the poet's imagination drives him on through "Bajdary" (X), a "beautiful valley through which the traveler generally proceeds to the southern coast of the Crimea" (Mickiewicz' own footnote). The rapidity with which words, phrases, and images succeed one another in this sonnet expresses the turbulence and violence associated with a state of "transitus": "I liberate my horse to the wind and don't spare the whip;/Woods, valleys, rocks turn and turn about, throng,/At my feet they flow, perish like the waves of a torrent;/I would stupefy myself, drunken with this whirlpool of images." Even the poet's horse, like the boat in Sonnet III, acquires the added significance of a symbol in this context; it may be read as the poet's own special talent that carries him through the chaos and darkness.

But the desire for oblivion which comes upon the poet at this stage of his journey is not granted. No matter how earnestly longed for, his intellect or higher self must oppose the desire. There is no oblivion or rest for the creative imagination. The poet must continue his pilgrimage through the landscapes of symbol.

As though to reward his perseverance in the quest, the landscape suddenly takes on a new aspect in "Alushta by Day" (XI). The gloomy and forbidding mountains, the storm-tossed seas and sombre ruins that thronged the first half of the cycle now yield to a landscape that is humanized: "Now the mountain shakes misty fleece from its bosom,/Golden corn resounds like a morning prayer,/The woods bow down and scatter from their green hair/ Rubies and garnets. . . ." By implication the landscape is no longer alien to the poet but is related to him by its human aspects. The integration is not, however, total or lasting. Further away a "locust stretches its winged shroud." This insect, the traditional "scourge of God," heralds hostile forces in nature, to which the poet now turns his gaze: "Yonder, a bald cliff gazes at itself in the waters,/The sea tosses and, hurled back, rushes forward again;/ In its roar, light plays as in a tiger's eyes,/Portending a still fiercer storm. . . ."

"Alushta by Night" (XII) opens in a blaze of light which is extinguished as the "lamp of the world" sinks behind the cliffs of Chatyrdag. The "errant pilgrim looks around him, listens." All his senses are brought into play: "In the valleys the night is mute,/ The fountains murmur . . ./The air breathing scent, the music of flowers,/Speaks to the heart in a voice enigmatic to the ear." The pilgrim falls asleep "under the wings of silence and obscurity." But sleep in Romantic poetry, and in the work of Mickiewicz especially, is not a mere state of rest. Sleep is a territory bordering on the unconscious mind, and we may expect signals from beyond that frontier. In this sonnet, the poet is awakened by the "dazzling flashes of a meteor," which flood the sky, earth, and mountains with a "golden deluge." We are reminded of the "flash that has revealed/The invisible world" in Wordsworth's *The Prelude* (VI, 601-2). As in the earlier sonnets, Mickiewicz does not make his symbolic meaning explicit. Indeed, a feature of the sonnets is the poet's avoidance of the explicit. This may be called a part of Mickiewicz' poetic technique.

In Sonnet XIII, the Mirza addresses the mountain Chatyrdag in the hyperbolic manner that sets his utterances apart from those of the pilgrim and the poet: "Trembling, the Moslem kisses the feet of thy rock,/O mast of the Crimea, great Chatyrdag!/O min-

aret of the world! O Shah of mountains!" He meditates on the
awe-inspiring indifference of the great peak to the fate of man;
and the imagery and diction heighten the unearthly, inhuman
impression exerted by the scene.

Next, in Sonnet XIV, the pilgrim speaks, as he gazes down into
a "land of abundance and beauty" which recalls to his mind the
"murmuring forests" of Lithuania, past time, and past love. By returning in memory to the landscapes and associations where his
emotional life began, the poet is adumbrating one of the major
themes of his later work: the remembrance of things past. This
theme was to renew and revitalize Mickiewicz' imagination in his
last great work, *Pan Tadeusz* (1834).

In "The Road over the Chufut-Kal Abyss" (XV), the Mirza
warns the pilgrim:

> Do not look yonder! The eye plunged
> As into the well of Al Kahir does not reach the depths.
> Do not even point your hand—you have no wings;
> Nor let your thought plunge, for the mind like an anchor
> Plunged from a tiny boat into the immeasurable depths,
> Will fall like a thunderbolt. . . .

In falling, the mind will "overturn the boat into an abyss of
chaos." The Mirza, with his knowledge of these symbolic regions,
is well aware that the psychic process of descending into the
abysses of the unconscious always threatens to overwhelm the
human ego. The unplunged depths of water within the abyss are
the unplunged depths of the mind, and their significance is made
still clearer in the pilgrim's reply: "O Mirza, yet I have looked!
Through the fissures of the world/There I saw—but what I saw I
will tell—after death,/There is no word for it in the language of
the living." He has experienced one of those rare moments in human life which opens up for an instant the ultimate abyss of the
mind, and he is totally unable to put the experience into words.

The Mirza makes his last appearance as guide and adviser in
"Kikineis Mountain" (XVI). This time he urges the pilgrim to
look down into the abyss. In Sonnet XV he had warned him not
to look down, so we may suppose that the abyss of the unconscious is no longer so terrible. Yet it is still remote:

the firmament lying below
Is the sea: amidst the waves the bird-mountain seems
Pierced by a flash to have stretched out wings
In a circle wider than the arch of a rainbow,
And to have covered the blue field of water with an island
   of snow.

The rainbow, which reappears in the final sonnet, is often symbolic of the bridge over chaos leading to integration and fulfillment of the personality. In this sonnet, however, Mickiewicz does not use the rainbow for this purpose; nevertheless it is there, on the edge—as it were—of his mind.

Yet the journey is still not ended. The Mirza adds: "Let us halt, the abyss underfoot,/We must leap over the ravine at full gallop." As earlier, the pilgrim's horse is his unique talent, which will carry him to safety over the last critical "ford." Significantly, in view of his symbolic function, the Mirza needs no horse, but will leap: "When I disappear from sight, look at the edge of that cliff,/If a lightning-flash gleams there, it will be my turban;/If not, men must not travel that road." The Mirza has guided the pilgrim past the abysses and peaks, and his purpose is completed, although even his last words carry a warning with them.

The pilgrim continues his journey in "Ruins of a Castle at Balaklava" (XVII). The contrast between a lost Age of Gold and the present day, when men are "more vile than the serpent," provides the sonnet with a structural pattern: "Let us climb the tower! I seek the traces of a coat of arms;/Here's an inscription, the name perhaps of a hero,/Once the terror of armies, now slumbering in oblivion,/Enfolded like a worm by the foliage of vines." He finds Athenian engravings, and he ponders over the Romans who hurled back the Mongol hordes here. But today "vultures with black wings encircle the tombs,/As in a city destroyed by the plague/The banners of mourning wave eternally from the bastions."

In the final sonnet, "Ajudah" (XVIII), the poet-pilgrim has attained the cliffs. The view no longer holds terrors for him as he contemplates the waves below "As foaming billows now in black ranks/Crushed together burst, now like white snows/They revolve superbly in myriad rainbows." He has surmounted the often terrifying flood of feeling and the unconscious content that threatened to overwhelm him during the journey. The chaos in his soul has been given meaning and order by art. Just as the waves, in ebbing from the shore, leave behind pearls and corals, so in the poet's own heart "Passion often arouses dangerous tempests,/But when you raise the lute, it flees/Harmless, to plunge into a torrent of oblivion,/And lets fall in flight immortal songs."

IV *Beyond Rational Frontiers*

Mickiewicz' *Crimean Sonnets* express in a highly individual and original manner an attitude toward nature that is characteristically Romantic and at the same time "modern." Nature itself is regarded as an experience in its own right—one that the poet himself undergoes and one that has the power to effect upon him certain psychological changes. Yet, in a way that is still not easy to understand and can perhaps never be fully understood, these changes are themselves projected into and mirrored in nature and its landscapes. Nature takes on symbolic significance; but, because this significance *is* symbolic, its full meaning must always lie beyond our ability to fathom. Mickiewicz himself may or may not have known what the sonnets "mean," and it would be absurd presumption to hope that we can understand them fully by analysis or that we can extract their deepest significance by paraphrase. Yet Mickiewicz is clearly pointing a way for us to follow him beyond the frontiers of the rational. He was the first poet in Polish literature to explore supra-natural experience in the language of symbols.[8] That he was conscious or at least intuitively aware of succeeding in his attempt in the *Crimean Sonnets* is evident from Sonnet XVIII, which comes, not as a logical deduction from what has gone before, but as the termination of an experience.

One question remains: why did Mickiewicz choose the sonnet form to give utterance to this kind of almost uncommunicable experience? The sonnet, after all, is characterized primarily by the strict, even rigid pattern of its metrical scheme. There is always the danger that, in the hands of an unskilled poet, his thoughts will be distorted at least slightly as he forces them into the pattern. He will be guilty of "clothing" his thoughts in language instead of expressing them as poetry.

But in the hands of a poet with something urgent to communicate—and what could be more urgent than psychological experiences of this kind?—the rigid structure provided Mickiewicz with a framework to control the strong contrasts, the chaos and darkness that formed his poetic material. Even so, he sometimes exerts a great deal of pressure on the framework by the way he handles technical details of caesura, rhyme, enjambement, and the like; but the technicalities cannot be discussed in a language other than the poet's own.

CHAPTER 4

Narrative Poetry

NARRATIVE poetry attracts little critical interest today; indeed, the narrative poems of Scott, which established the popularity of the genre early in the Romantic period, have few admirers at present. Most people who read poetry at all find lyrical poetry more immediately rewarding. However, nearly all the Romantic poets, from Keats to Lermontov, attempted the genre.[1] Mickiewicz did so twice, and his interest in narrative poetry as a literary genre is attested by his translation into Polish (1832-33) of Byron's *Giaour* (1813).

I Grazyna

The first of Mickiewicz' narrative poems were *Grazyna,* published in the second volume of the *Poems* (1823). A remarkable feature of the poem is its length (1090 lines), and the fact that Mickiewicz spent some three years in composing it. The poem was conceived and executed as a sustained exercise; and, as such, it occupies a place in the development of Mickiewicz as a poet similar to that of *Endymion* in the development of his contemporary John Keats. Both poets were approximately the same age when they began their poems; and the act of prolonged willpower each poet had to make in struggling with what was, for both, unrewarding material, led in both cases to a "breakthrough" preparatory to a great advance in control and maturity. Narrative poems enabled the young poets to extend the technical mastery of their art, to distinguish between poetic themes that vitalized their imaginations and those that resisted their efforts. *Grazyna* and *Endymion* were trials of the "power of the Imagination" and of invention.

The length of *Grazyna,* for all its value as a sustained exercise, mitigated against its artistic success. The desire to compose a long poem led Mickiewicz (as it had led Keats) into structural difficulties he was unable, despite prolonged efforts, to solve in a satisfactory manner. At the same time, from his labors over *Grazyna,* Mickiewicz learned one of the basic principles of all Romantic narrative poetry. He perceived that such poetry sets out to tell a story in a special way, and that this "special way" of presenting a narrative is primarily a matter of technique.

Technique in narrative poetry, as in the novel, consists largely in the writer's being equipped with certain stratagems or devices that he exploits for a specific purpose. These stratagems include an ability to tell the story for certain different "points of view." Sometimes we hear the poet himself speaking within the poem as he explains or comments on what is happening, or tells us why characters behave as they do or what they are feeling. He may also intrude to draw our attention to some significant or mysterious detail. Elsewhere in the poem, the poet may disappear, allowing us to overhear his protagonists speaking or thinking to themselves; yet again, the poet may choose to present incidents through the eyes of one of his protagonists, perhaps using the present tense to give an impression of dramatic actuality and to induce in us a sensation of being present. Another variation sometimes used to indicate a shift in point of view is a protagonist or character who stands apart from or outside the action and comments or ponders on its meaning.

The primary function of these strategic shifts in perspective is to prevent the poem's readers from forming a fixed or objective attitude to the characters or incidents presented. The poet's aim is to involve us in the narrative by deliberately mystifying us or by arousing our curiosity, and hence to generate in us as we read a subjective feeling towards the poem. This aim explains why the story, or plot, in nearly all Romantic narrative poems is usually baffling: we are left in the dark about the characters (who are often haunted by mysterious secrets), about their relationships, their past lives, their intentions, and even about the full significance of events that occur. In addition to asking "what happens next?"—which all story-tellers want us to ask—we ask all kinds of other questions as well; and, by doing so, we acquire a measure of subjective involvement with the poem.

Another function of the shifts in point of view characteristic of this kind of poetry is one of which the poets may or may not have been fully conscious. The obscurity of plot may in itself enable him to skirt over or round weak points in his narrative, such as implausible chronology or characterization, or improbable coincidences.

Mickiewicz drew the matter of *Grazyna* from the history of medieval Lithuania, when the country was parcelled out between a number of minor principalities and dukedoms. The ruler of one such principality was Litawor, whom Mickiewicz chose as a protagonist in the tale. *Grazyna* opens in a way traditional to Romantic narrative poetry:

> The darkness increases, a north wind chills,
> Below—a snow storm, on high the moon
> Amidst a moving torrent of black clouds
> Showed in the gloom but part of its eye,
> And the world was shaped like a vaulted edifice,
> And the sky shaped like a moving vault.

Three knights on horseback ride into this landscape, and Mickiewicz identifies them as Teutonic Knights, the rapacious enemies of the Lithuanian principalities in the fourteenth century. They are seeking Litawor, and Mickiewicz now shifts the poem's perspective to show us Litawor himself in his gloomy castle. A few lines later, we are given the anticipated reference to Litawor's "secret" and to the "Gloom of his furrowed brow,/His compressed lips, the lightning flash of his eyes/And the stern bitterness of his countenance." Litawor, on hearing that the three knights have arrived, gives mysterious orders that torches be lit throughout his castle and that trumpets be sounded to awaken all his knights. An extended and cryptic dialogue ensues between Litawor and his councilor Rymwid.

The poem's heroine, Grazyna herself, is not mentioned until the poem is half over. She is Litawor's wife, in whom "The charms of a maiden and of a matron/Were wonderfully combined in one person." Mickiewicz expatiates, in poetic diction heightened by archaisms and involved syntax, on Grazyna's virtues:

> Despising the needle and spindle, women's pastimes,
> She adopted a sterner weapon;

[63]

Often, a huntress on her Samogitian steed,
In a garment of rough bear-skin,
. . . Returning from the field, she would deceive the eye,
And sometimes servants in the court-yard,
And would receive tribute due to the Prince himself.

On hearing that war is impending, Grazyna hastens to her husband's chamber—and another significant shift in point of view
occurs. Mickiewicz conveys the scene between husband and wife
through the medium of Rymwid, who listens at the keyhole and
overhears "A dialogue ever more agitated and confused,/Now it
slowed down, was more difficult to hear,/Most often the lady
spoke, very rarely the Prince./He was silent, sometimes seemed to
laugh. . . ."

Finally, the essential conflict around which the poem is constructed begins to become less obscure. Litawor's "secret" is that
he has entered into an agreement with the Grand Master of the
Teutonic Order against his kinsman, Duke Witold. Litawor is, in
a word, placing self-interest against the common good of Lithuania as a whole; and Grazyna cannot accept her husband's plans.
Without telling him, she leads the Lithuanian troops against the
Teutonic Knights; and she perishes. We are given to understand
that Litawor commits suicide on her funeral pyre.

As with many narrative poems by other writers, Mickiewicz was
clearly restricted by a plot into which he had somehow to cram
all the other elements—characters, setting, and the poetry itself.
Grazyna is additional evidence—if any is needed—that this
method is not conducive to successful art. Despite passages
striking enough in themselves, *Grazyna* does not merit more
detailed attention than has been given it.

II   Konrad Wallenrod

The technical accomplishment which Mickiewicz acquired in
writing *Grazyna* is also evident in *Konrad Wallenrod*—another
narrative poem, which he wrote in 1828, toward the end of his
stay in Russia. The poem's sub-title is "A Historical Tale from
Lithuanian and Prussian History"; and its epigraph announces the
poem's theme: "You must know there are two ways of fighting—

a man must be both wolf and lion" (Machiavelli). The wolf is traditionally associated with cunning and treachery; the lion, with courage and strength. We may expect to find these qualities embodied in the main protagonist, Wallenrod.

Mickiewicz furnished the poem with a prose preface suggesting its historical background. Once again, we are back in medieval Lithuania and the Duchy is under attack by the Teutonic Knights. But (Mickiewicz adds) "several centuries now conceal the incidents narrated here . . . Lithuania is entirely in the past: her history presents a happy subject for poetry in that the poet, singing the events of those times, need concern himself only with the historical subject, an investigation of that matter and artistic production, without referring to the aid of his readers' interests, passions or decorum." By thus insisting that his poem dealt exclusively with the remote past, Mickiewicz hoped to avert the attention of the tsarist censorship from the allegorical meaning of the poem.

The plot, a common one in Romantic narrative poetry, concerns an individual caught in a moral dilemma; and Mickiewicz handled it in such a way that he could exploit to the full all the mysterious aspects of his central protagonists and the events in which they are involved. These events are as important as the protagonists, and Mickiewicz takes an introduction, six cantos, and copious historical and other footnotes to unravel their complexities. We know from *Grazyna* that the complexities of plot are not primarily intended to baffle: their function is to ensure our interest and to arouse an emotional or at least subjective attitude.

The time of the action is stated in the following lines: "A hundred years had passed since the Teutonic Order/First waded in the blood of Northern pagans. . . ." The year is therefore 1390, and the Germans are in arms on the Lithuanian frontier:

> The Niemen divides the Lithuanians from their foes:
> On one side gleam the towers of temples
> And the forests murmur, dwelling-place of the gods:
> Across the river, a cross—the emblem of the Germans,
> Erected on a hill, hides its head in the sky,
> Stretches out its arms, threateningly, towards Lithuania.

In Canto I, "The Election," Konrad Wallenrod makes his appearance in the ancient seat of Marlborg, seat of the Teutonic Knights. For "General agreement among the Brotherhood/Sets Wallenrod above all the rest." Mickiewicz dwells on Wallenrod's enigmatic character, his mysterious past, and his eccentric behavior. He is described as "a foreigner" among the Knights, but he is respected because he is celebrated in battle and tourneys—and because "The great Christian virtues adorn him:/Poverty, modesty and contempt for all the world." He shuns courtly life, elegance of diction, and graceful manners; and he is capable of being powerfully stirred by certain words which arouse "passionate feelings in him": "the homeland, duty, the loved one,/Mention of the Crusades and of Lithuania." Like Litawor, Wallenrod also possesses a deep and unexplained secret, which is evidently shared by an old bard, or minstrel, Halban, who exerts a mysterious hold over him.

In Canto II, Wallenrod and the aged minstrel are contemplating a tower located near the city. An "unknown, pious female" has found in the tower "an anchoret's hiding place." Mickiewicz leaves us in doubt whether she was "inspired by Heaven in her enterprise, or wished to relieve the pangs of conscience by the balsam of repentance." His description of the tower and the lady entombed within it is interspersed with rhetorical questions (which do not expect or receive an answer), intended to intensify our curiosity and wonder at her fate.

As Konrad passes by the tower, the lady addresses him:

Thou art Konrad, O Heavens! the decrees have come to pass,
Thou shalt be Grand Master and shall slay them!
Do they not recognize thee? In vain thou conceals't it,
Even though like a serpent thou acquire another form
Yet much of the former man remains in thy soul.

Halban and the Knights present interpret this speech as a prophecy that Konrad should be elected Grand Master of the Order, a rank recently left vacant. Left alone, Halban sings the first of the "Songs" with which Mickiewicz sought to vary his method of narration. Halban celebrates in ballad-form the unhappy love of a Lithuanian girl for a "foreign youth." This significant epithet has already been applied in the poem to Wallenrod himself; but, in accordance with the principles of his narrative technique, Mickiewicz leaves us to divine or to be baffled by its precise meaning in his story and in relation to the poem's protagonists.

Konrad again wanders by the anchoret's tower in Canto III and holds "important discourse" with her. She bewails her fate in the "Song from the Tower":

> Three fair daughters had my mother,
> And I was married first of all;
> O happy youth, happy existence,
> Who told me there is any other joy?
> O handsome youth! Why dids't thou tell me
> That which no one in Lithuania knew before?

A long verse dialogue follows between Wallenrod and the anchoret in her cell; and Mickiewicz implies, by the way they address one another, that they are, or were at one time, in love. But Wallenrod declares: "I tore myself away/For ever and ever from your embrace/When I voluntarily died to happiness/To undertake deeds of blood. . . ." He informs the lady that the Teutonic Knights are soon to declare war "against the walls of Wilno" under his command. However, he is deliberately postponing the campaign for his own mysterious reasons, which Mickiewicz prefers not to elucidate at this stage in the narrative.

Canto IV is "The Banquet." Wallenrod heads the company as host to Duke Witold of Lithuania, "formerly an enemy, now guest of the Order." Witold has entered into alliance with the Knights against his own homeland. Wallenrod's attitude towards the feasting is one of contempt: "leaning on his elbow,/ He listened with contempt to the unseemly discourse."

During the course of the banquet, an aged bard in Witold's retinue sings, to the accompaniment of a lute, the "Song of the Lithuanian Bard." Briefly, the elaborate plot, the theatrical figures, the poetic diction and rhetoric that largely constitute the poem are forgotten. Poetry comes to life as the bard celebrates the folk songs of his native land and their significance as an "arc of the Covenant between past and present," which remains unbroken as long as the folk honor and respect their own poetry. Mickiewicz is here reverting to one of the themes which always vitalized his creative imagination: the power of poetry in human life and its force in national tradition. He expresses his feeling for this theme in words which generate poetry by their meaning, rhythm, associations, and context:

> Flame may devour painted history,
> Robbers plunder treasures by the sword,
> The song will survive intact, a crowd will assemble;
> And if abject souls cannot nourish the song
> With grief, or nourish it with hope,
> It will adhere to the ruins
> And thence will tell of ancient times.

The bard follows his song at once with a "Tale," in which Mickiewicz makes a bold experiment in meter. Like other Romantic poets, notably Coleridge in *Christabel,* Mickiewicz seizes upon the opportunities that the flexible form of the narrative poem offers to vary his method of narrating whenever possible. The "Tale" is written entirely in unrhymed hexameters: these are lines containing six metrical feet and six stresses placed regularly across a varying number of syllables (ranging from thirteen to seventeen). The meter is extremely difficult to use in English, though Coleridge attempted it as a technical feat (but not for any intrinsic poetic value the meter may possess): "In the Hexameter rises the fountain's silvery column." Goethe and Schiller also employed the meter in lyrical poetry.

But the use of hexameter verses in Polish is a technical achievement that surpasses in difficulty its use in English, German, or the Classical languages where it originated; for the stress in a Polish word falls almost without exception on the penultimate syllable. Like French, Polish verse is traditionally patterned on the number of syllables in a line, not on the number of stresses we hear; and the lines are held together by the reinforcement of rhymes occurring at line-ends. Mickiewicz' success in maintaining this elaborate and difficult meter for some three hundred lines is a measure of the technical versatility he had by now acquired.

The "Tale" advances the poem's mysterious plot a little further. The bard tells how a Lithuanian child named Walter was kid-

napped by Teutonic Knights and brought up with the name of
Alf. As a young man, Alf-Walter fled the Knights and took refuge
in the Lithuanian town of Kowno; there he met and married Aldona, a daughter of the Grand Duke. She was "as young and
beautiful as a good divinity." Soon the Germans were besieging
Kowno. Alf, who has retaken the Lithuanian name Walter that he
originally bore, tells Aldona that he alone knows how best to defeat them. After commanding her to forget him, Walter rides
away to put his words into action. As he departs, Aldona's eyes
fall upon a nearby tower. With this significant hint in our direction, the "Tale" ends.

A "great stir" arises in the banqueting hall. Only Wallenrod

> Sat silent with bowed head,
> Deeply moved, seizing often
> A goblet of wine, he quaffs it to the dregs.
> In his attitude a new change is seen,
> Varied feelings in sudden flashes
> Cross his fevered countenance.

So moved is Wallenrod that he, too, sings, this time a ballad "Alpuhara," the matter of which is drawn (so Wallenrod tells his
hearers) from his own war experiences in the mountains of Cas-
tille. The last king of the Moors, Almanzor, is defending the town
of Alpuhara from the Spaniards. As a last desperate resort, the
king infects himself with plague, then surrenders to his enemies,
and spreads the disease among them. Like the bard's tale and
song, Wallenrod's ballad is intended to illustrate an aspect of the
poem's theme: heroic self-sacrifice for the good of the homeland.
As verse, the ballad is closer to eighteenth-century imitations than
to the genuine folklore ballad, or even to Mickiewicz' own early
ballads of 1822.

Not until Canto V, "The War," does Mickiewicz begin somewhat to clarify his plot and to reveal what lies behind his characters' behavior. Wallenrod now leads the Teutonic Knights into
battle against the Lithuanians; a pause follows; then months later
he returns to Marlborg, defeated: "All was lost, Conrad had lost
them all." A German spy discovers that "the man called Konrad
Wallenrod/Is not Wallenrod./Who is he? No one knows. . . ."

The Teutonic Knights, realizing that Wallenrod's vulpine treachery has betrayed them, condemn him to death. Canto VI, "The Farewell," depicts Wallenrod at the anchoret's tower. She is revealed to be his long-lost spouse Aldona, and he himself is the Alf-Walter of the bard's tale. He implores Aldona to emerge, but she refuses and dies as the poem ends.

III *Plot in Poetry*

The faults in *Konrad Wallenrod*, as in *Grazyna*, are largely due to its plot—the reason the plot has been dwelt on here at some length. Minor deficiencies such as anachronisms, geographical and chronological inaccuracies in the text have been exposed by various critics; but these can be attributed to poetic license and are of little relevance to the poetry itself. Besides, they are partially concealed, unless we look for them, by Mickiewicz' artful manipulation of perspective. As a conscious literary artist, Mickiewicz must have been aware of these inconsistencies and would have improved them if he could. But narrative poetry does not expect a very close look from its readers. The poet expects us to become so involved in his poem that we overlook inconsistencies or accept them.

Mickiewicz' insistence on dominance of plot had a more damaging effect on his presentation of character. His protagonists were conceived to fit into the plot, and they are directed by the poet as they parade through heroic, pathetic, or sentimental scenes. The preconceived plot left Mickiewicz little or no room in which his imagination could expand and transmute the unrewarding facts of history into art. Besides, we may even inquire whether attempts to portray "characters" are a poet's business at all, or whether he should not leave them to novelists and playwrights. Be that as it may, Mickiewicz' critical acumen and taste must have made him well aware that the "plot" is the last element to be considered in poetry. What must come first is the poetry and the meaning. These concepts should shape a plot, rather than be shaped by it. That Mickiewicz grasped this principle is evident in the long poetic novel *Pan Tadeusz* (1834), which is crammed with poetry from beginning to end and is hardly at all concerned with a formal "plot line." But in *Grazyna* and in *Wallenrod*, Mickiewicz was versifying dead subjects, and the poems reveal this fact in their tone and structure.

The political allegory which may be read into Wallenrod need not concern us here. The poem has been variously interpreted as an inspiration to revolt, as a warning against revolt, and as a tragic picture of the consequences of revolt.[2] But these intepretations have nothing to do with the poem as a work of literary art.

CHAPTER 5

Forefathers' Eve
Part III

THE third and last part of the poetic drama *Forefathers' Eve* appeared in 1832. This part of the work is only tenuously connected in theme and subject with parts II and IV published a decade earlier in Mickiewicz' first book. Part III (so called merely because it was published third in sequence) is the most complex, the most enigmatic, and the longest and the most famous of the play's three parts. Mickiewicz demonstrates in it once again the compulsion he shared with a number of contemporary poets, to express himself in a long, if fragmentary work. *Forefathers' Eve*, Part III, takes its place within the framework of the whole drama as a synthesis of poetry, music, and gesture—elements dear to the Romantic spirit.[1]

For the materials out of which he erected his poetic edifice, Mickiewicz went back to certain incidents in his own life dating from 1823, when he and other young members of the Philomat secret society were arrested and imprisoned in Wilno by the Russian authorities. Mickiewicz selected this comparatively everyday occurrence—hundreds of young Poles underwent such experiences throughout the nineteenth and twentieth centuries in Poland under Russian domination—and used it to construct an individual and national myth.

I *Personal Mythology*

As myth, *Forefathers' Eve*, Part III, has its own gods, its own rituals, its own moral laws. Mickiewicz' striving to create a mythological system of his own is, of course, typically Romantic in character. The ultimate significance of much Romantic poetry, after all, lies in the way poets tried to create their own myths. They were intensely aware that the old gods of mythology had lost their power; yet human nature felt, and still feels, a deep need of the peculiarly healing and vitalizing power of myth.[2] Somehow, as Jung has shown, the human spirit needs mythology to supply an outlet for the inexhaustible energies of the human unconscious. Mythology provides, in a way that is still not clearly understood, symbols that help carry the human spirit onwards. Such symbols cannot be manufactured or invented; they seem instead to be the spontaneous production of the human mind, and can only be organized by art.[3]

One of the myths of Classical antiquity that retained something of its validity for Romantic poets was the story of Prometheus. In 1773, Goethe (whom Mickiewicz met and admired) produced fragments of a drama in which Prometheus symbolized the free spirit of a creative artist rejoicing in his powers. The fragments were not published until 1830, and we cannot know whether Mickiewicz read them. Byron's drama of 1816 depicts Prometheus as a symbol of heroic individualism in revolt against human and divine tyranny. Both Byron and Goethe went back for a source to the *Prometheus Bound* of Aeschylus (fifth century B.C.), whose protagonist was a benefactor of mankind who sought to intercede for man with the Gods, but suffered harsh punishment at the hands of Zeus, a despotic tyrant. Mickiewicz' emerging vision of himself as the spiritual leader of his nation, suffering equally unjust punishment at the hands of the tyrannical and despotic Tsar Alexander of Russia, gave the Prometheus myth personal relevance. Indeed, we know that for a time Mickiewicz considered embarking on a poetic drama about Prometheus to express his own concept of the myth.

Instead, Mickiewicz chose to project his own personal tragedy and, by giving it the element of objectivity which dramatic form provides, to externalize it. We need not, therefore, regard *Forefathers' Eve*, Part III, as being entirely an expression of Mickiewicz' personality. He was dramatizing experience which may or may not have been imaginary, and it is not our concern to differentiate.

The play has a prologue, nine scenes, and a terminal sequence of six long poems about Russia. These poems, the "Digression," constitute a second act or epilogue. In the dramatic part of the work, Mickiewicz uses all the conventions of playwriting: exposition, preparation, situations, contrasting characters and scenes, reversals, climaxes, and denouements. However, Mickiewicz could not accept the conventions of Classical tragedy, which prevailed in the Polish theater until the 1830's. In consequence, he was faced with the herculean task of imposing on his contemporaries a new literary form which would be valid for expressing his myth. The literature of the nineteenth century is full of such attempts, from Goethe's *Faust* to Hardy's *Dynasts* (1903); and all display to a greater or lesser degree what Middleton Murry called a "true creative impulse, working free from the discipline of an accepted form, producing huge, unwieldy works of genius." [4] But the drama was the literary genre (apart from the still rudimentary novel) that allowed Mickiewicz to present in the most effective way all or any manifestations of human nature.

As well as the mythical and symbolic level, the play also has a realistic one. In part, it is a chronicle, depicting a number of Mickiewicz' contemporaries in recognizable "real" settings and involved in incidents which really happened. The characters range from several of Mickiewicz' university colleagues in Wilno to Novosiltsov, the Russian Governor-General of Lithuania responsible for their imprisonment, and eminent figures in Warsaw society at the time. We know that Mickiewicz had been strongly impressed by the popular chronicle plays of two now forgotten French dramatists, whose plays blended satire and contemporary events for the delectation of Parisian audiences. Mickiewicz' enthusiasm for these *hériodrames* (as they were called) is an example of a great artist who elected to treat his subject according to a passing trend of literary fashion. What aroused his enthusiasm for the *hériodrames* was most probably the opportunity the genre afforded for presenting the poet's own views on the political and social realities of his time. Like most Romantic poets, Mickiewicz was profoundly occupied with such affairs.

Another literary genre which Mickiewicz adopted for his own purposes in writing *Forefathers' Eve*, Part III, was the opera libretto. He knew such operas as Mozart's *Magic Flute*, the forerunner of Romantic opera, and Weber's *Freischütz*, its epitome. From the study of the libretti of these and other operas, Mickiewicz discovered how a skilled librettist like Da Ponte was able to eliminate situations of low dramatic content, and to provide occasion for the arias, duets, and concerted numbers which constitute an opera. Just as the opera composer uses the theater to glorify music, Mickiewicz employed it for the glorification of poetry.

II Levels of Meaning

Forefathers' Eve, Part III, is a proverbially enigmatic work, like *Hamlet* or *Faust*. A vast amount of commentary and speculation has grown up around it. But no final conclusions can be reached on the play, nor does any single interpretation satisfy all its readers, because no "meanings" are explicitly stated in the text. Instead they are presented and acted out by the characters in their setting. Through these elements and through the poetry we acquire a sense of manifold meanings. The play's wealth of meaning is one significant reason for its power.

The action of *Forefathers' Eve*, Part III, takes place in three worlds: in the subjective cosmos of Mickiewicz' own thoughts, feelings, and private mythology; in the subjective world of Wilno and Warsaw in the year 1823; and, finally, in a metaphysical world ruled by non-human forces. The poet's tasks in handling this complexity of levels were to ensure that none became too ethereal or too real and to maintain an equilibrium between them all.

The play's central figure is Gustav, a young prisoner. His name at once relates him to the pathetic and love-sick ghost of Part IV. Shortly after the play begins, however, Gustav is transformed into Konrad—another highly significant name in the work of Mickiewicz for it is associated with the heroic traitor Wallenrod. Moreover, a tentative identification may be made between Gustav-Konrad and Mickiewicz himself. By carrying the identification a step further, the fate of Konrad acquires the allegorical meaning of an inspired poet imprisoned and rendered mute by the tsar, and is thus emblematic of Mickiewicz' entire generation and hence of Poland itself.

But the story of Konrad and the story of Poland are not two separate things: neither is merely a background to the other. In the same way, Konrad is significant as himself, as a literary construct representing an individual, as well as in his symbolic function. Other characters partake likewise of symbolic meaning while playing their parts in the drama as protagonists.

A second central character is Father Peter. As a priest, he stands for the powers of good and of purity. He is Konrad's friend, adviser, comforter, and teacher of revealed wisdom. He is also a messenger endowed with prophetic gifts. He represents knowledge, reflection, insight, and moral qualities such as goodwill and readiness to help, all of which are characteristics of the wise old men of myths and legends.[5] As the play proceeds, we begin to discern that Father Peter and Konrad, in addition to being themselves, can also be regarded as two aspects of the same person, divided into two roles for dramatic purposes and corresponding to two sides in the poet's own personality and (by extension) of ours. One side (Konrad) rebels but is forced to submit to the other, and the play ends with a reconciliation of the opposing sides.

The third main character is Governor-General Novosiltsov, an embodiment of the Tsar himself. The latter does not appear in person, though we are made vividly aware of his presence. As a symbolic representation of the dominant powers of evil, tyranny, and fear, Novosiltsov provides the drama with its darker aspect. By setting up a tension of oppositions between these three main protagonists, Mickiewicz generates a potential which brings the conflict to life.

The metaphysical world of the play is represented by various supernatural phenomena, which range from the appearance of angels and demons to dreams, visions, and nightmares. The use of these elements does not imply that Mickiewicz "believed" in the supernatural and occult, any more than Shakespeare did when he created the ghost of Hamlet's father. The supernatural constituents of *Forefathers' Eve*, Part III, are evidence that Mickiewicz, like twentieth-century man, was fascinated by any kind of manifestation emerging from the depths of the human psyche. In his day, such manifestations were expressed by an interest in such non-rational modes of perception as mesmerism, a power supposed to be exerted by the "inner man."[6] Other preoccupations included dreams, now recognized as the products of unconscious psychic activity and as one of the most direct methods

of approaching what Jung called "the world of inner experience."
Essentially, however, Mickiewicz' purpose in introducing these
elements into his play was to admit his belief that the supernatural and the irrational are significant in human life. He was as
powerfully convinced as John Keats of the mysterious kinship
which exists between sleep, dreams, and poetry.

III *The Intent of Part III*

As was his custom, Mickiewicz preceded *Forefathers' Eve*,
Part III, with a prose introduction which explains something of
the play's background and authenticates the action to be un-
folded on the stage. He claimed that his play "contains but a few
lesser hints of the huge image" of what had been happening all
over Poland: he is to present "a few incidents drawn from the
persecutions initiated by Tsar Alexander." In 1822, the Tsar and
his creature, Senator Novosiltsov, began a campaign aimed at
the systematic destruction of the Polish nation. The entire country was transformed into a "vast prison." After describing how
Novosiltsov "put to torture the children and young men of Poland," Mickiewicz claims that there was "something mystical,
enigmatic" in the Wilno incidents that he himself participated
in and that form the subject of his play. Yet his purpose in writing *Forefathers' Eve*, Part III, was not to incite hatred among
his fellow countrymen for their enemies, nor to awaken the pity
of the rest of Europe. Modestly, the poet merely claims that he
was seeking to preserve a "true memory" of a few months in the
history of his nation. The play has, therefore, no conventional
plot or intrigue. The prologue and nine scenes do not demonstrate the different stages of a story, nor the development of
character. Instead, they present and illustrate aspects of Mickiewicz' central themes.

The Prologue

After Biblical epigraphs from the tenth chapter of St. Matthew,
which prepare us for the religious current that imbues the play,
the curtain rises on the Basilian monastery in Wilno, now converted into a political prison. A prisoner is asleep in his cell;
like Byron's prisoner of Chillon, he at once embodies for a Polish
audience enslaved nationalism.

While the prisoner sleeps, his Guardian Angel speaks to him as a "disobedient, unfeeling child." But as it is in the natural order of things for a child to grow and develop, we may expect this order to be apparent in the play. The Angel has had insight into the mind of the prisoner throughout his earlier life: "When night rocked you asleep/I would stand over your passionate dream/Like a white lily/Crouching over a muddied spring." Sometimes the Angel led the child's soul in dreams into a region "where eternity glows"; at other times he appeared to him as a a "Hellish monster" to terrify his soul. Then the prisoner's soul would awaken

> As though night long it had been at the source
> Of oblivion, drinking its dregs.
> Then you drew down the recollection of higher worlds
> Like a waterfall when it flows
> Into an underground cavern, drawing with it leaves and flowers.

As in the *Crimean Sonnets*, the symbols here are indicative of the processes which occur within the human psyche. The prisoner's dreams reflect both the heights of spiritual good and the depths of evil and terror that lurk within his mind. But all his dreams have sunk back into the depths and have been forgotten.

The Angel draws attention to the hidden significance of these dreams by telling that the prisoner's mother, now in Heaven, would ask the Angel "What sort of dreams did my son have?" Unnerved, the prisoner awakes and looks out his cell window at the dawn. He speculates on the nature of dreams and on those that trouble him:

> But dreams?—Ah, that silent, speechless, mysterious world,
> The life of the soul—is not that worthy of man's inquiry?
>
> . . . . .
>
> Wise men say a dream is but a recollection—
> Accursed sages!
> Do I not know how to distinguish dreams from memories?
> Will they persuade me that my imprisonment
> Is but a memory?

Again he falls into a fitful sleep, but Mickiewicz has made it clear that this is no ordinary sleep. Instead, it is a purposeful process, the aim of which is to draw together all the assets of the prisoner's psyche and to induce a state of receptivity in which he will become responsive to psychic manifestations.[7]

Nocturnal spirits are heard from right and left—those on the right are traditionally benevolent spirits; those on the left, the embodiments of evil. An angel tells the sleeping prisoner:

> We have prayed to God
> To render you into the hands of your enemies.
> Solitude is the handmaiden of wise men,
> And you, in your solitary imprisonment,
> Like a prophet in the wilderness,
> Ponder your destiny.

The two opposing groups, as in medieval mystery plays, also represent the conflicting sides in man's nature: "God and the devil are in combat, and their battlefield is the heart of man" (Dostoevsky).

The Angel's voice penetrates into the prisoner's sleep as a prophetic dream: "You will be free, we have come to tell you so." At this the prisoner wakes again, and the voice is still audible in his mind:

> I am to be free—yes! I know not whence the news,
> Yet I also know what it is to be free by the mercy of a Muscovite.
> The scoundrels will remove the chains from my hands and feet
> But will seize my soul—I shall be exiled!
> Wandering in a throng of foreigners, of enemies,
> I, the singer—and no one will understand my song.

His outburst ends with a significant simile: "Alive, I shall be dead for my homeland,/And my thought will lie closed within the shadow of my soul/Like a diamond contained in unclean stone." The symbolism of diamonds concealed within dirt to represent a human soul held captive is well attested in world literature.

For all his psychic receptivity, however, the prisoner is still incapable of receiving revelation. He has yet to pass other thresholds than that of sleep. As the prologue draws to an end, the prisoner rises to his feet and inscribes with a fragment of charcoal:

"Gustav died November 1823." Opposite this, he writes: "Konrad born here, November 1823." This moment is of great psychological import. Like other heroes of myth, Gustav-Konrad has been reborn.[8] The change of name, profoundly significant, symbolizes the pagan "rite of passage" and Christian baptism. Both ceremonials are exercises of severance; the individual's mind or soul is radically divided from the life he is leaving behind. The individual has died to the past and has been reborn to the future. Natural man returns from the rite as spiritual man. The self-centered Gustav of *Forefathers' Eve*, Part IV, has voluntarily undergone rebirth; and, by investing himself with another name, he has, by the same token, invested himself with another personality. In adopting the name of Konrad for his protagonist, Mickiewicz hints strongly at an association with the name Wallenrod—a character who placed his country above personal love or happiness. The transformation announces, therefore, another central theme of the play.[9]

On another level, the dramatizing of a spiritual death and rebirth expresses a final break with the Age of Reason from which Gustav was struggling to free himself in *Forefathers' Eve*, Part IV. The rational attitude to the irrational processes of the human mind, dominant through the Age of Enlightenment, became meaningless to Gustav; and his rejection of that age was expressed in his isolation. Similarly, the pilgrim of the *Crimean Sonnets*, passing alone through the landscapes on his "night sea journey," symbolizes a voyage of exploration into regions of the human mind that the rational writers of the eighteenth century refused to enter—or even to admit their existence. The Gustav of *Forefathers' Eve*, Part IV, resembled that other great figure of early Romanticism—Goethe's Werther, who lacked the psychic stability required to survive in the Waste Land. Mickiewicz' pilgrim attained stability through his symbolic journey to integration by the help of his art. Konrad, as the third variation on this archetypal character in Mickiewicz' poetry, finds the power to endure in an enlargement of his personality.

Enlargement of the human personality, as Jung has indicated, is a psychic phenomenon which springs very often from a process of rebirth within the individual's life.[10] Konrad undergoes this rebirth and is therefore a stronger, more integrated personality than his earlier self (Gustav). After rebirth, Konrad is also in a state of heightened spiritual receptivity; he is, therefore, prepared for revelation. The powerful Biblical association cannot be overestimated, for Christ Himself was twice born through the rite of baptism.

Moreover, it is psychologically appropriate that Konrad's rebirth takes place within a dark cell, a place corresponding to the cave, that traditional place of rebirth in myth and in literature. The darkness symbolizes that of the unconscious which, being hypothetical, can never be brought into the light and seen. Konrad takes his place with other tragic and prophetic figures who retreat into cells or caves for psychic purposes; in this context, Timon of Athens, Prospero in *The Tempest*, and Zarathustra come to mind. In every case, a retreat into the individual's self is implied.

The reborn Konrad sinks almost at once into a state of sleep. This interval of retirement from the world always follows a rite of passage. Once again, his ego descends into the underworld of the unconscious psyche in preparation for the critical moment when it comes upon him: when he will be required to exert all his spiritual, intellectual and physical powers. A Spirit comments on the significance of what has just occurred: "O man! If you knew your power!/When the thought in your mind, like a flash within a cloud/Will gleam unseen, clouds gather/To create a fertile rain or thunderclaps and storms." The Spirit concludes: "Humanity! Each one of you might, though alone, imprisoned,/ Overturn or elevate thrones by power and faith." The silent, interior drama of the Prologue is followed by the first scene which is realistic, even noisy.

Scene I. *A corridor. An armed guard nearby. Several young prisoners with candles leave their cells. Midnight.*

It is Christmas Eve; and apart from the symbolic associations of this day, it was also the anniversary of Mickiewicz' own birth. Each of the young prisoners bears the name of one of Mickiewicz' contemporaries who had been imprisoned with him in 1823. The dialogue is quick, full of exclamations, greetings, slang. They enter Konrad's cell which is revealed "as in the prologue." The name of Senator Novosiltsov is first mentioned by Thomas

Zan, who explains to his young companions that the reason for
the mass arrests in Wilno is

> that Novosiltsov has arrived here from Warsaw.
> You must know the Senator's character.
> You know he has been out of the Tsar's favor,
> That he has drunk and squandered the profits of his earlier booty,
> Has lost his credit with merchants and is at his last resort
> For, despite his utmost efforts and devices
> He cannot track down in Poland any conspiracy;
> So he has decided to visit a fresh territory—Lithuania,
> And has come here with all his general staff of spies.

Gradually the language used by the prisoners acquires a heightened, more emotional pitch; and a climax is reached with the long
monologue of Jan Sobolewski, which gives an account of events he
witnessed that morning while being escorted back to the jail
after interrogation. Mickiewicz is making use of the Classical
device of tragedy in which events that cannot be depicted on
the stage are presented in the form of an extended report by a
messenger or other figure. The incidents Sobolewski saw and
now describes are essentially real, factual, even "true"; but Mickiewicz uses poetry to imbue them with the "mystical, enigmatic"
atmosphere he referred to in the preface. Not that Sobolewski's
language is in any way self-consciously "poetic"; on the contrary,
the diction is plain, the words are close to prose order, and the
images are revealing and relevant to the context in which they
occur. Sobolewski vouches for the truth of his account in his
first words: "I saw this myself. On returning, I asked the cor-
poral/To stop: he permitted it a moment. I was standing far
off,/I hid behind the pillars of a church. In the church/Mass
was just being held." Suddenly all the celebrants of the mass
hasten from the church and surround the adjacent prison "like a
motionless rampart": "From the prison gates to the square, as
at some great rite,/Armed troops with drums stood in two rows;/
In the center, Black Marias. I watch, from the square comes/
The chief of police on horseback." The contempt and the irony
that now enter Sobolewski's tone are conveyed by hyperbole:
"From his look you'd easily divine/He's a great man, and is to
celebrate a great victory,/That of the northern Tsar, the con-

queror of—children." With the appearance of the Polish children,
Sobolewski's irony gives place to a different tone:

> behind each came a guard with bayonet drawn,
> Young boys, wasted, all like recruits
> With shaven heads:—their legs chained.
> Poor boys! The youngest, ten years old, poor creature,
> Complained he could not move his chain;
> And pointed to his bloody, naked leg.
> The chief of police rides up, asks him what he wants;
> The chief of police is humane, he himself examines the chain:
> "Ten pounds, in accordance with the required weight."

Among the children and youths is Janczewski, whose attitude
towards his captors is rendered by Sobolewski's comparing him
to Napoleon gazing from an uninhabited cliff with "an eye
haughty, dry and tranquil."

When the carriages bearing the young prisoners set off on their
journey into exile, Sobolewski says: "If I forget them, do You,
God in Heaven/Forget me." As the last carriage disappears,
Sobolewski concludes:

> I glanced into the empty church and saw the priest's hand
> Raising the Body and Blood of our Lord,
> And I said: O God, You who spilt innocent blood
> By Pilate's sentence for the world's salvation
> Accept this childish sacrifice by the Tsar's sentence,
> Neither so holy nor so great, but equally innocent.

A "long silence" follows the climax and end of Sobolewski's
narrative. Gradually the emotional tension generated by the
speech is allowed to relax as the prisoners continue their dialogue and Jankowski sings a blasphemous song. Konrad, who
has been silent and pondering during the entire scene up to this
point, also sings; then, to the accompaniment of a flute, he begins to improvise in poetry. The music activates his imagination,
and symbolic images are spontaneously created. Konrad sees
himself rising above humanity to the rank of the prophets. He
is endowed with supra-normal powers and can see the "Sybilline
book of the future destinies of the world." He has transcended

the level of consciousness and entered a world of almost cosmic proportions. He will return to it in the next scene; in the meanwhile, symbols begin emerging:

> There, below!
> Look, look, future events and coming years
> Like little birds, when they see an eagle,
> Me, an eagle in the sky!
> See how they fall to earth and flee away.

Konrad becomes this eagle; he is endowed with the eagle's eye "of lightning," which is often symbolic in Romantic poetry of insight and intuition, and with eagle's talons, with which he will seize the birds of time. For an instant Konrad breaks off; then he queries,

> What's this? a bird has risen and is spreading its wings,
> It veils them all, it challenges me with its eye;
> It has wings as black as a storm-cloud,
> Broad and as long as the shape of a rainbow.
> And it is covering the whole sky.

Still in his state of hallucination, Konrad addresses this huge black raven and seeks to establish its identity by questions and challenging boasts:

> It's an immense raven—who are you?—who are you, raven?
> Who are you? I am the eagle!—the raven stares—it entangles my thought!
> Who are you? I am the Thunderer!
> It stared at me—it struck me in the eyes as though with smoke,
> It confuses, it entangles my thoughts—

Alarmed by Konrad's cryptic utterances and pallor, several prisoners interrupt and seize him. Protesting he has challenged the raven, Konrad falls to the ground. The prison guards are heard returning; there is a hurried exchange of dialogue between the others; then all hasten back to their cells and Konrad remains alone.

As the Angel prophesied in the Prologue, Konrad has been

rendered into the hands of an enemy, the black raven, which emerged from the depths of his mind while he was in a state of trance. This bird, the traditional emblem for evil, was also used more specifically as the symbol of political enslavement by Polish Romantic writers. But, like all birds and cold-blooded creatures, the raven also functions in Konrad's vision as the symbol of an alien psychic world he must challenge or be destroyed. Had his companions not interrupted him, the raven's "wings as black as a storm-cloud" would have engulfed him. An even clearer symbolism of this kind is presented by the whale Moby Dick, which destroys Ahab. Mickiewicz knew, as well as any twentieth-century psychologist, the grave dangers inherent in psychic states.

The bird symbolism in Konrad's "short improvisation" (as it is called) is "true" symbolism in that it is essentially impervious to any final, rational interpretation. For this reason, all the symbolism in *Forefathers' Eve*, Part III, despite its imperviousness to logical explanation, exerts a powerful effect on audiences and readers. Mickiewicz instinctively chose symbols (or was furnished with them by his imagination) that provoke and arouse what lies buried in the unconscious of all men.

Scene II. *The Great Improvisation*

The "improvisation" was a favorite literary form of Romantic poets, and Mickiewicz himself was persuaded to improvise at evening parties for friends. Perhaps the chief advantage of the form was that it enabled the poet's imagination to find immediate expression. Genuine improvisation was direct utterance, existing in its own right and not in any way tampered with or polished. Such poetry, emerging from within the poet (who was often induced into a trance-like state by music) was not produced by industry or application; it came to him directly in the form of spontaneously generated images. The Symbolists of the late nineteenth century, who inherited much from the Romantic movement, adopted the method as a means of venturing deeper into the unconscious with the aid of more sophisticated techniques. A renewal of interest by poets in the improvisation occurred among the Surrealists of the twentieth century. They went still further and often relied exclusively on "chance" (automatic writing, computers) for the expression of voices emerging out of the undetermined regions of the human mind, for which they only served as mediums.

While Konrad's Improvisation in Scene II seems to exhibit all the characteristic features of the genuine, spontaneous improvisation, it is in reality a highly organized, controlled art. But Mickiewicz brings into play all the immense technical skills he possessed to create the impression of a spontaneous outburst of poetry. Even the meter, with its abrupt variations in pattern, contributes strongly to the impression of emerging feeling and imagery that resist as they emerge.

Konrad's rebirth in the Prologue has, as might be anticipated, revealed a self who is no longer a mere individual but a Poet. His improvisation, appropriately, is preceded by a "long silence," during which we may suppose that various elements within him are at work. His psychic energies then begin to flow, his creative imagination again transcends the level of ordinary everyday consciousness, and poetry begins to emanate from the dark, hidden part of his mind. This process is expressed by images and symbols of the unconscious: underground rivers, invisible torrents of rushing water, the depths of the sea, volcanoes, and the flashes of lightning that cast momentary illumination on the depths. His power of expressing this process in the form of poetry has not been acquired

> from the Tree of Eden
> From the fruit of knowing evil and good,
> Nor from books or legends,
> Nor from solving puzzles,
> Not from magical studies,
> I gave birth to myself as creator,
> Hence came my powers. . . .

The significance of the rebirth is here made explicit. This deep, strong emotional experience widened enormously the range of his personality and his imagination and uncovered creative forces within him that were hitherto dormant.[11]

But these powers cause Konrad to magnify and exalt his new "self." The encounter with these powers within the self, which emerge after a rebirth, is known to be an overwhelming experience—some individuals who have experienced it regard it as divine revelation. Now Konrad finds he can place his hands upon the stars and force them to revolve; he can play upon the stars as if they were glass globes that, when touched, emit the music of the spheres. Konrad is laying claim to a power hitherto reserved to the unknown and unseen beings of Classical and Renaissance philosophy, who produced this music and performed the "world concert" of celestial harmony. Konrad's power also endows him with love—a transcendental love:

> But this love of mine is for the world,
> My love rests not on one individual alone
> Like an insect on the flower of a rose:
> Not on one family, not on one century.
> I love my entire nation!—I have embraced
> All its past and future generations,
> I have pressed them to my bosom,
> Like a friend, a lover, a spouse, like a father.

Gustav's "natural" love of Part IV has been ennobled and exalted into a different kind of love altogether. Yet, significantly, Konrad seeks to impart his boon on his own nation alone; he is not the Messiah, bringing a message to the whole world.

Such power corrupts in addition to ennobling. Konrad claims the right to rule human souls and demands that the Almighty Himself abrogate His supreme powers; this aspiration was Lucifer's original sin, and it brought about his downfall.

> Give me government over souls! I so despise the dead edifice,
> Which the communality call the world and are wont to praise,
> That I have not yet tried whether my word
> Might not instantly overturn it . . .
> I want authority, give me it, or show me the way to attain it!
> I have heard there were prophets, rulers of souls,
> And I believe it: but what they could do, so can I,
> I want authority such as You possess,
> I want to rule souls as You rule them.

His demand is met by silence, the most conclusive reply to any demand and one against which there can be no appeal. Yet Konrad persists, this time "with irony":

You are silent, silent! Now I know, I have studied You,
I have comprehended what You are and how You rule.
He who called You love was a liar,
You are but intellect.
People learn Your ways by intellect, not heart. . . .

Another silence provokes Konrad into asserting that feelings, life,
death, time, and eternity are but "a spark," a "moment." He challenges the Almighty again, now without irony; he is aware that
he is not alone but is one with a great nation, that he and his
homeland form an entity: "My name is Million—because I love/
And suffer punishment for millions."

When there is still no answer, though voices to left and right
comment enigmatically, Konrad utters his third challenge:

Speak—for I will aim against Your nature;
If I do not reduce it to ruin,
Then I will cause the entire realm of Your kingdom to tremble;
For I will cast my voice into the whole compass of creation:
This voice, which goes from generation to generation;
I will cry aloud that You are not the father of the world, but . . . .

At this point, we hear the voice of the Devil, which completes
Konrad's phrase with the words: ". . . The Tsar!" Now Konrad
understands why his challenges were met with silence: God's
place has been seized by the Tsar, abetted by the Devil. Konrad's
psychic powers forsake him; he falls into unconsciousness like a
medium who, unknown to himself, has been uttering truths that
come from his own hidden depths.

The obscurities in Konrad's improvisations are within the tradition of all prophetic literature, from the Bible to William Blake
and (in Poland) Zygmunt Krasiński. Many critics have attempted
to explain and interpret the improvisations, but they remain as
cryptic as ever. The more we look into them, the more manifold
are the significances they yield. The "Great Improvisation" of
Scene II, with its extended flow of highly symbolic poetry, is
particularly esoteric: this poetry is not immediately intelligible
and can perhaps best be approached as one of those experiences
in which critical "knowing" has little or indeed no part.

As Konrad falls, spirits to the right and left are heard again as they battle for the possession of his immortal soul. These spirits represent forces that rush to take possession of any individual unless they are warded off by eternal vigilance. In this respect, they are acting within the framework of Catholic theology, which is also represented in *Forefathers' Eve* by the Catholic practices of confession, absolution, and exorcism. On hearing the cell door open to admit Father Peter, the Bernardine monk, the spirits fall silent. Father Peter's role in the myth is that of the helper endowed with supernatural powers who assists the mythical hero to survive his trials. On a different level, he is also the embodiment of Christ, who has come to redeem Konrad, the Christian Prometheus.

Scene III

Father Peter announces his allegiance immediately: "In the name of the Father, the Son and the Holy Ghost." He is accompanied by the Corporal and a prisoner. On hearing voices in Konrad's cell, the Corporal realized something was amiss and hastened to bring the priest. All three react differently to Konrad's state of trance: Father Peter senses the presence of Evil, the Corporal is uneasy, and the prisoner believes Konrad a victim of epilepsy; today we might say that Konrad is the victim of a neurosis or worse. Konrad speaks incoherently:

> The abyss—a thousand years—empty—very well—still more!
> I will endure ten thousand thousand times—
> To pray? here prayer serves no purpose—
> Was there ever such an abyss without end and limit?
> I did not know—yet there was.

Father Peter proceeds to exorcise the evil spirit by forcing it to manifest itself so he may then expel it: he is practicing a traditional form of psychotherapy:

> Unclean spirit, I know you by your poison,
> You are here again, the slyest of all satans,
> Again you creep into a deserted house, filthy serpent.
> You have crept into his mouth, you have crept to destruction here,
> In the name of the Lord, I have seized you,
> *Exorciso* . . . .

The evil spirit is made manifest. But instead of being sinister or monstrous as we might expect, it proves grotesque, even droll. It speaks in a "babble of tongues"—French, German, English, Spanish—and claims to be called "Lucretius, Leviathan, Voltaire, Old Fritz, Legion." Like Goethe's Mephistopheles, this evil spirit is the humorist who makes all things vain and worthless by scoffing. It is worldly, sardonic, contemptuous, witty, and cruel; its laughter, as Bergson might have said, is that which is "incompatible with compassion." It is a monster because it holds up to scorn and mockery the voice of true faith:

> I will speak to you of the past and the future.
> Do you know what they say of you all over town?
> (*Father Peter prays*)
> Do you know what will become of Poland in two hundred years?
> And do you know why your prior does not encourage you?
> And do you know what the Beast means in the Apocalypse?

There ensues between Father Peter and this creature an argument between a man with a deeply religious nature and the spirit whose function is to deny and mock. But Father Peter's faith, expressed in the age-old ritual formula of exorcism, forces the spirit to yield and depart. As soon as it has gone, Konrad comes to his senses and speaks to Father Peter:

> You elevate me! Who are you? Beware, you yourself will plunge into this valley.
> He gives me his hand—let us fly! I fly like a bird—
> I breathe pleasant perfume—I am alight with flames.
> Who gave me his hand? Good men and angels;
> Whence this mercy that brings you to descend to me in the valley?

Konrad is still at a low level of consciousness, like all mediums when they emerge from a trance. He is unaware of what has happened and cannot identify his saviour, Father Peter. When the two meet again under different circumstances in Scene VIII, Konrad is not at all sure who Father Peter is; he merely senses they may have met "in a dream."

Father Peter urges Konrad to pray because "the hand of the Lord has touched you"; then he falls into an attitude of total abasement: "Lord, here am I, Your servant of old, an old sinner,/

A servant worn-out and unworthy./Make this young man into the servant of Your faith,/And I will take upon myself all the punishment for his sins." A Christmas song is heard from the adjacent church, and choruses of angels join in as the scene ends.

Scene IV. *A country house near Lwow*

Midnight has struck, and a young girl Eva is at prayer in her room. She prays for family and country, then for the young men whose martyrdom Mickiewicz has shown in the preceding scenes. As Eva falls asleep, angels sing; and she is visited by a dream. Hers is a dream of life, and Mickiewicz renders its meaning by the symbolism of flowers, rainfall, and bright sky. The Virgin Mary and Child appear to her, and Eva's wreath of flowers comes to life: "The rose, this rose, lives!/A soul has entered into it./ It moves its head gently,/What fire comes from it!" This brief scene provides a powerful contrast to what has gone before and exemplifies the way Mickiewicz uses contrast throughout the play for structural purposes. To contrast two scenes or two characters in drama always implies a relationship between them that contributes to structural coherence.

Eva's dream again introduces the element of music into the play. Introduced by a chorus, the dream relates to opera and, more specifically, to the aria. This composition is in two movements that represent moods of contrast: the first part (*cavatina*) is *andante* and represents serenity; the second (*cabaletta*) is *allegro* and represents, as here, feelings of joy and exultation.

Eva does not appear again, but she is an important element in the play's meaning. Is she the goddess of all myths, the incarnation of promised perfection? At all events, Eva is certainly a heroine of Romantic drama who stands for the essential rightness of instinct as opposed to the critical intellect. Eva's mind is in harmony with her instinctive religious faith, as was that of Goethe's Margaret. The hero's mind, on the other hand, is profoundly at odds with faith. Again the principle of contrast is in operation.

Scene V. *Father Peter's cell*

Father Peter is at prayer in the same attitude of total abasement before the Almighty as in Scene III. As before, he emphasizes that he is dust and naught before God; but, even so, he will venture to address Him. A vision comes to him:

A tyrant has arisen—Herod! O Lord, all Poland's youth
　　Rendered into the hands of Herod.
What do I see?—long white Ways of the Cross,
Long roads—without end—through wilderness and snow,
All to the north! There, there in a distant region
　　They flow like rivers.

Some of the exiles enter into "a gate of iron"; others, into "rocks and caverns." Father Peter asks God how this can be, whereupon a child appears in the vision: "Behold! a child has emerged—it grows—it is a defender,/The resurrector of our nation—/From an alien mother: his blood is of ancient heroes,/And his name will be forty and four." We can only speculate on the meaning of this oracular vision, the identity of the redeemer, and the use of numbers to name him. The language of visions, like the language of dreams, does not have the clarity of conscious language. Not, however, that Father Peter's vision is difficult in the sense that Konrad's improvisations are. The enigmatic numbers "forty and four" used to express the name of the coming redeemer of Poland have been read as possessing some undefined cabbalistic traditional meaning, but no one has been able to state precisely what it is. Another suggestion is that Tsar Nicholas II, the forty-fourth king of Poland, is meant (Krzyżanowski). Forty has Biblical associations: the Israelites spent forty years in the wilderness, the Flood lasted forty days and nights, Moses passed forty days and nights on the mountain, and Christ was seen forty days after the Crucifixion. The number four (quaternity) was discussed as a totality symbol by Plato, and experienced by Ezekiel in the vision of four seraphs. Christian metaphysics recognized four Persons in the Trinity (plus the Devil). In analytical psychology the four parts of a circle symbolize the unity of human personality. Moreover, numbers themselves play an important if mysterious part in all mythology.

Father Peter beseeches God to hasten the coming of this redeemer; then he realizes that, before this event can come to pass, Poland herself must undergo crucifixion. The Biblical analogy is carried to its inevitable conclusion. At the moment of Poland's death and martyrdom, angels sing an Alleluja, and resurrection follows. The predestined deliverer appears:

> He is the commander of freedom made visible on earth!
> It is he who will erect on glory the vastnesses
> > Of his church!
> Elevated above men and above kings,
> He stands on three crowns, himself without a crown:
> > And his life will be the labor of labors,
> > And his title—man among men.

Mickiewicz underscores the enormous contrasts between Konrad's improvisations and the two visions of Eva and Father Peter, respectively, by means of a radically different selection of words. Konrad's improvisations are centered upon himself and what is happening within; he therefore expresses himself in what we now call "symbols of the unconscious." Eva's vision of the Virgin and Child, light and flowers, is uttered in the language of innocence and instinctive faith. Father Peter's vision, which he sees and experiences as an appalled observer but in which he does not participate actively, is in the language of Biblical revelation.

Scene VI. *A magnificent sleeping chamber*

Mickiewicz exploits the dramatic possibilities of contrast (between characters, scenes, and language) yet again, as we see the senator tossing and turning in bed, "sighing." He is Novosiltsov, the Russian Governor-General responsible for carrying out the tsar's repressions and persecutions in Lithuania. Two devils hang over his head, waiting for him to fall asleep; then they will pounce like birds of prey upon a sparrow and "claim his dreams." Beelzebub himself joins them, declaring he has the tsar's authority for the two devils to torment the senator. These devils are as ludicrous and grotesque as the evil spirit which Father Peter exorcised in Scene III. Their presence also suggests that, like Konrad, Novosiltsov is obsessed by a neurosis.

The senator falls asleep and dreams aloud. His dream, like all dreams, is alarmingly "true" while it lasts:

> A letter? For me—From his Imperial Highness the Tsar!
> In his own hand,— ha ha ha! a hundred thousand roubles.

A decoration! where . . . footman, pin it on—here.
       The title of Duke!
   Ah! Ah! Grand Marshall: ah! they will burst with envy.
              (*he turns over*)

A moment later Novosiltsov is at the tsar's court and is advancing through a crowd of fawning courtiers who hate and fear him: "Ah, what agreeable murmurings,/Agreeable murmurings all around:/The Senator is in favor, in favor, in favor, in favor." Everyone bows to him, he is the "soul of the gathering" as "They gaze at me, they envy me—I turn my nose up./O delight! I am dying, dying of delight!/(*he turns over*)."

His restless movements as he sleeps herald in, as before, another section of the dream. The tsar himself enters: "But! What's this? He doesn't look at me, he frowned—he looked away?/Ah! Your Highness! Ah! I can't speak—/My voice has died—ah! treambling, sweating—ah! the trembling chills, freezes me." The courtiers take their example from the tsar and turn away from the senator, whispering and deriding him: "They avoid me. Ha! How empty, mute./The Chamberlain is a scoundrel, a scoundrel! See him bare his teeth—/Faugh! that smile has flown into my gullet like a spider./(*he spits*)." Malicious epigrams fly round his head like wasps, and, still asleep, he tries to drive them away. But the words fly into his ears "like crickets," and the Imperial court becomes a collection of insects, birds and snakes:

   What rustlings! The courtiers hoot like owls,
   The ladies' trains hiss like rattle-snakes,
   What horrible noises! Laughter! Uproar!
The Senator has fallen out of favor, out of favor, out of favor, out of favor.

              (*he falls out of bed to the floor*)

Senator Novosiltsov betrays his kinship with the evil spirit that possessed Konrad in Scene III by the highly grotesque nature of his dream. Its symbolism reveals that the senator is committed to a world that is contemptuous, cruel, and witty; there cruelty and falsehood provide the values by which the inhabitants live. The imagery of insects and cold-blooded creatures in his dream indicates the presence in his mind of alien psychic

[94]

material. He is suffering from a profoundly disordered personality wracked by the powers of evil. The devils take possession of him as he sleeps on:

> Now we will rend his soul from his mind, as though loosening
> A mad dog from its chain: but not completely, we will muzzle it,
> Leave it half within his body, so he shall not loose his feelings;
> We shall fly with the other half to the world's end,
> Where the temporal ceases and eternity begins.

They will bind the senator's soul (or psyche) on the frontier of Hell and the human conscience, and torment him until "the cock crows thrice, and we must bring back/The weary and polluted soul from its torment;/ Fasten it once more to his mind as to a chain,/And once more enclose it within his body as in some filthy kennel." This short scene reveals yet again Mickiewicz' intuitive awareness of the workings of the unconscious and its relation to dreams.

Scene VII. *A Warsaw drawing room*

The action of *Forefathers' Eve*, Part III, moves in Scene VII from Wilno to the capital of the Grand Duchy of Warsaw. High government officials in the Russian administration, "eminent writers," ladies of fashionable society, generals, and staff officers are having tea. In a recent Polish production of the play, these persons were depicted as rigid, wax-like effigies; and, in contrast to them, another group is shown standing by the door. This group consists of young men and two older Poles, who are conversing in a spirited manner. The stage directions add that the persons at the tea table speak French, but those by the door speak Polish. We are reminded of the grotesque evil spirit of Scene III with its command of tongues, and we recognize Mickiewicz' point in respect to the eminent and fashionable characters in the drawing room.

There is no contact between the two contrasting groups. While the young men and the two Poles by the door speak of the recent deportations and trials in Lithuania, the ladies and gentlemen at the tea table converse frivolously about fashionable balls. One lady complains that "Since Novosiltsov left Warsaw,/No one has been able to give a smart party;/I haven't seen an elegant ball once./He knew how to arrange a picturesque ball." Her mention of the senator arouses laughter among the gentlemen and echoes the laughter and derision Novosiltsov heard in his dream in the preceding scene.

Meanwhile, at the door, one of the young men refers to Cichowski, who has recently been set free after a long imprisonment. He is persuaded to give an account of Cichowski's sufferings, much to the consternation of those at the tea table, one of whom remarks: "It is not very safe even to hear such things,/But to leave in the middle would be impolite." He takes his leave instantly, but the others approach the young man (Adolf Januszkiewicz) and listen: "I knew him as a child: he was young then,/Vital, witty, merry and famed for his charm;/He was the life of a party: wherever he appeared/He entertained us all with tales and witticisms." [12] Shortly after his marriage, however, Cichowski disappeared; when his cloak was found on the river bank, he was generally believed dead. Three years passed:

> One evening
> Prisoners were brought to the Belvedere palace from a monastery
>   prison.
> It was a dark and rainy evening; I know not whether by chance
> Or deliberately, but someone witnessed this procession,
> Possibly one of the courageous young men of Warsaw
> Who investigate the location and names of prisoners.

He shouted over a wall to the prisoners, asking their names; and a hundred names were heard, including that of Cichowski. His wife was immediately informed: "She wrote, she hastened there, she begged, she beseeched,/But apart from the name—she heard nothing more." Three more years passed without trace or news, but in the meantime rumor in Warsaw declared that Cichowski was still alive and refused to confess, although "For many nights he was not allowed sleep,/He was fed on salt fish and refused drink;/He was dosed with opium, terrified by monstrous hallucinations." But soon further waves of arrests occurred in Warsaw, and Cichowski was forgotten again, except by his wife:

> Until, not long ago, they rang one night at his wife's house—
> The door opened: an officer and gendarme with rifles,

And the prisoner. It was he. They ordered pen and paper;
She had to sign that he'd been returned alive from the Belvedere.
They took the signature and threatened him: "If you
Betray . . ." and did not finish. They left as they had come.

Januszkiewicz hastened to see the ex-prisoner, only to be warned
that he would be watched by a spy if he did. Finally he succeeded
in meeting with Cichowski: "They said it was he, for I did not
recognize him./He'd grown stout, but with a hideous stoutness;/
Vile food and decayed air had bloated him;/His cheeks were
puffy, turned yellow and livid." He refused to speak or to recognize Januskiewicz until the latter identified himself:

Then he stared at me and studied me.
Ah! Everything he had suffered in his daily torments,
Everything he had brooded over in his sleepless nights,
I discerned it all momentarily in his eyes:
For there was a terrible veil over his eyes,
His pupils resembled fragments of glass
That are found in the barred windows of a prison,
Their color grey as spider-webs,
And which, when seen obliquely, gleam like the rainbow;
And in them are seen blood-red rust, sparks, dark patches,
But which the human eye cannot penetrate through.

A month later the narrator again visited Cichowski, thinking to
find an improvement in his state:

But so many thousand days he'd been under the pressure of
        interrogation,
So many thousand nights held discourse with himself,
So many years the tyrants had interrogated him under torture,
So many years listening walls surrounded him:
And his only defence had been—silence,
And all his company—darkness;
That the cheerful city had failed
To erase in a month the lessons of those many years.

Despite all Januskiewicz' efforts to persuade his friend to tell
the history of his imprisonment—"the history of all the heroes of
Poland" in Siberia, in fortresses, and in prisons—Cichowski could
not:

He had forgotten. His memory, engraved upon
Like a Pompeian book buried underground, had turned to decay:
Its resurrected author himself could not read it,
He only said: "I will ask the Lord God,
He recorded everything, he will tell me all."
(*a long silence*)

This narrative is related by contrast to Sobolewski's monologue in
Scene I, which expressed heroism and courage. Januszkiewicz' account, however, depicts heroism of a different order, which ends
in psychological collapse and resignation.

The eminent writers at the tea table break the long silence to
discuss Januszkiewicz' narrative as material for literature. They
represent the coterie of Classical poets in Warsaw, whose disapproval of Mickiewicz and of the new Romantic writers is satirized
by exposing their preconceived ideas about poetry. One declares:

People listen to such tales, but who will read them?
And, I pray, how is one to describe contemporary events:
In place of mythology, we have eye-witnesses,
Then it's a clear, holy rule of art
That poets must wait until . . . until . . .

Another offers a different opinion:

It would seem to me
That it does no harm at all if the topic is new:
Unfortunately, though, it is not Polish, national.
Our nation loves simplicity, admires hospitality,
Our nation dislikes terrible, violent scenes;—
To sing, rather, the flirtations of rural lads,
Flocks and herds, shadows—we Slavs love the idyll.

Yet another protests there can be no poetry without a court to
judge the taste and beauty of a poem—and there is none in Warsaw.

Indignant and contemptuous, the young men leave the drawing
room. Mickiewicz puts the final words of this scene into the mouth
of Wysocki, a Polish officer who took part in the 1830 Warsaw
Insurrection against the Russian occupants: "Our nation is like
lava,/ Cold and hard, dry and repulsive on the surface,/But a

hundred years will not quench its inner fire;/Let us spit upon this dry crust and penetrate to the depths."

Scene VIII. *His Excellency the Senator*

Scene VIII, the play's penultimate one, is the longest, and the most theatrically varied and striking. The action has returned to Wilno and to a vestibule in Novosiltsov's apartments. This setting refers back to the prologue and to early scenes in the Wilno monastery prison and provides a framework for the intervening scenes.

From the vestibule one door leads to the interrogation chamber and another to the senator's private suite, from which music can be heard. The time is "after dinner," visitors are playing whist, and the senator himself is taking coffee, surrounded by members of his entourage—Chamberlain Baikov, Pelikan, and a doctor. Guards and footmen also populate the stage. Theatrically speaking, this setting is little more than a "neutral place" appropriate to the series of encounters that occur as the scene proceeds.

Using a grotesque and characteristic pot-pourri of Polish, Italian, and French, Novosiltsov complains to Baikov that people vex him, even at dinner parties, with anxious inquiries about fathers or sons imprisoned at his orders. Pelikan (a "real" character representing a notorious university professor in Wilno who ingratiated himself into Novosiltsov's favor) informs the senator that a young prisoner named Rollison has fallen sick after an interrogation during which he was beaten. The senator inquires how many lashes were given:

PELIKAN: I was at the interrogation, but no count was made.
Mr. Botwinko interrogated him.
BAIKOV: Mr. Botwinko! ha ha!
He's not slow to end, once the humor has him.
I vow he dealt with him pretty well—
Parions he counted out some three hundred strokes.

Novosiltsov's reaction is one of amazement and derision: "Trois cents coups et vivant? trois cents coups, le coquin;/Trois cents coup sans mourir,—quel dos de jacobin!" Finally the senator turns to Pelikan to inquire: "Did he confess?" Pelikan replies: "Almost nothing; he clenched his teeth,/Shrieked he did not want to accuse his innocent friends./But from these few words much is revealed —/Evidently his pupils are—his friends." The doctor hastens to add his contribution: "I was just telling/Your Excellency that young people are being infected with madness/In teaching them rubbish: for instance, ancient history!/Who of us doesn't see that this drives them mad?" He explains that by "ancient history" he has in mind lessons dealing with the "republics" of Athens, Sparta, and Rome.

A few moments later, a footman announces the arrival of two ladies who visit the senator's house every day, seeking an audience. One is the old and blind mother of the prisoner Rollison. She presents a letter from the Princess Zubov, Novosiltsov's mistress; and he is obliged, though reluctantly, to have her admitted.

The two ladies are accompanied by Father Peter. At first, Novosiltsov is civil; but soon his other personality shows through the mask. He threatens Mme. Rollison's companion: "You'd best stay home and watch your sons./Suspicion has fallen on them." When she turns pale, the senator bursts out laughing at her terror. Mme. Rollison, weeping, begs the senator to be merciful to her son: "Your Excellency! Mercy—I'm a widow! Your Excellency!/I hear they've killed him—is it possible, O God!/My child! The priest says he's still alive;/But they are beating him, Excellency!" Novosiltsov attempts to deny this charge, but Mme. Rollison has "a mother's ear" though she is blind:

> now all my soul is in my hearing,
> The soul of a mother . . .
> . . . at midnight the town is mute,
> I listen—at midnight, there by the prison wall—no, I am not
>   deceived;
> I heard him, I heard him—as God is in Heaven;
> I heard his voice with my own ears,
> Quiet, as though underground, as though coming from the center of
>   the earth.
> And my hearing penetrated the thick wall, deeply;
> Ah, it went deeper than the sharpest of eyes.
> I heard them torturing him.

She falls to her knees at the senator's feet just as one of his guests, a woman in a resplendent ball gown, enters from the inner apart-

ments. In her presence, the senator's attitude changes. From bully-
ing and deriding the unhappy Mme. Rollison, he moves to smiles
and promises. Giving Father Peter a penetrating glance, he agrees
to let the priest visit Rollison: "Very well, very well—so be it—
the Tsar is just/ The Tsar does not forbid priests, indeed he himself sends them/To revert young men to morality./No one appre-
ciates, loves religion as I do—/(*he sighs*)." He even promises to
review Rollison's case; but, as soon as Mme. Rollison and her companion have left, he rages at the footman who admitted them and
sentences him to a hundred lashes.

Next the senator questions Father Peter, who has remained
behind, and orders the secretary to make notes of what the priest
says "before witnesses." In an outburst of coarse joviality, he demands "how do you know/ What other people's children are doing
in prison?/Was it you who went to his mother with information?"
And Peter answers: "It was I." Novosiltsov then threatens Father
Peter with "the Russian knout" when the latter refuses to answer
further questions: "Do you know, monk, that I could hang you,/
And we'd see whether your prior could resurrect you. . . ." Father Peter's brief, tranquil words infuriate the senator, and he tells
Pelikan to strike him. At this point, Father Peter prophesies to the
doctor, who has also been taking part in this scene; "Today you
will stand before your Maker." A few moments later the doctor
discovers to his alarm that his watch has stopped at the hour of
twelve. As Father Peter warns him, "My brother, the Lord God
warns us in manifold ways."

The door leading to the senator's apartments and the ballroom
opens to admit ladies in gala attire and officials; music is heard; a
shift in mood occurs; and the next section of this scene is subtitled
The Ball—a scena, in the operatic sense of a concerted number
with soloists and chorus. As in Scene VII, Mickiewicz provides detailed stage directions for this scene: "On the left stand officials
and their spouses—on the right, some young men, a few young
Russian officers, some elderly gentlemen in Polish national costume, and several young ladies." When the guests take part in a
minuet, the senator dances with Baikov's fiancée, and Baikov with
the Princess.

The ball scene is related to the senator's nightmare in Scene
VI. As he dances the minuet, a buzz of malicious comments and

epigrams in the form of asides by various ladies and gentlemen in the minuet occurs:

A LADY: Look, look at the old man, how he writhes,
How he's wheezing—may he break his neck.
(to the Senator)
How beautifully, how lightly you dance!
(aside)
Il crèvera dans l'instant.
A YOUNG MAN: Look how he fawns and licks his lips,
Yesterday he committed murder, today he's dancing.

The musical quotation from Mozart's opera serves as preparation for a further reference to the same work. The orchestra stops for a moment, then strikes up the aria of the *Commendatore*. The solemn chords announce the arrival of the Stone Guest at Don Giovanni's banquet, who comes to bear away the don to Hell as punishment for his sins. Thunder is heard outside the senator's ballroom, the guests grow agitated, there is a shriek outside, and Mme. Rollison demands admission "in a terrible voice." She forces her way into the room and, although blind, advances upon the senator. He is momentarily petrified with terror, and she denounces him:

Where are you? I will find you, I shall smash your brains out on the
     pavement—
Like my son's! Ha, you tyrant! my son, my son is dead!
They hurled him from a window . . .
I felt his blood on the pavement—by the Living God
I sense it here—the same blood, my son's blood,
Someone here is bespattered with blood—his executioner is here, is
     here!

She advances directly upon the senator, who retreats. As Mme. Rollison falls in a swoon, a thunderbolt strikes a house on the university corner. Going to the window, the senator announces that the thunderbolt has struck the doctor's house; and Pelikan rushes in to reveal that the bolt has, in fact, struck the doctor dead: "The thunderbolt caught him in the inmost room,/ It damaged nothing except silver roubles, which melted,/The silver was lying on the desk, right by the doctor's head/And certainly served as a lightning-conductor." As one of the minor characters comments: "Russian roubles, I see, are very dangerous things . . ."

The thunderstorm continues, and the guests leave in alarm and dismay. The senator, alone with Father Peter and Pelikan, questions the priest: "Tell me now, little priest, do you cast spells,/ How did you foresee the thunderbolt? God's punishment, perhaps?" Father Peter replies by telling two "old but meaningful parables." The first describes travelers taking shelter from the heat under a wall. Among them is a murderer, whom an angel warns that the wall is about to collapse. He is saved while the other travelers perish; but, when the murderer thanks God, the angel warns him, "You have sinned most of all! You shall not evade retribution,/But will perish last, most notoriously, most shamefully!" The second parable relates that a Roman general defeated a powerful king; and all the king's men were put to death, save the king himself and his ministers. They rejoice until a Roman soldier explains that they are to draw the general in triumph through Rome. Then, "when you have been led in golden chains,/He will render you up to the executioner, and he will place you/In deep, underground, dark exile,/Where there shall be everlasting weeping and the gnashing of teeth." The king refuses to believe this; but, before Father Peter can bring his parable to an end, the senator loses interest and goes off the stage with Pelikan.

Now Konrad enters, accompanied by two soldiers who are bringing him from his prison cell for interrogation. He and Father Peter come face to face. Konrad stops dead and gazes at the priest:

> Strange, I never saw this man before,
> Yet I know him as though he were my own brother.
> Was it in a dream? Yes, in a dream, now I recollect,
> That same face, these eyes, I saw him in a dream.
> He it was, I think, who dragged me out of the abyss.

He addresses Father Peter and ceremoniously offers him thanks for "A mercy which only my conscience knows." Giving Father Peter a symbolic ring which the priest is to sell, Konrad instructs him that half the proceeds are for charity; the other half, for masses to be said for the souls in Purgatory: "I know what they suffer, if Purgatory is enslavement." In return for the ring, Father Peter offers Konrad some cryptic advice:

You will travel a long, unknown road:
You will be in a crowd of the great, wise and wealthy,
Seek out a man who knows more than they do;
You will recognize him, for he will greet you first in God's name.
Listen to what he tells you . . .

But before Father Peter can conclude his prophecy, the soldiers force Konrad to accompany them, and the scene ends.

Scene IX. *Forefathers' Eve*

The characters, setting and atmosphere of Scene IX echo Part II of the play, with which Mickiewicz had begun his monumental labors a decade earlier. He again uses a framework to provide some structural coherence to the whole work, but the coherence is one of form rather than of meaning since Scene IX has little apparent connection with what has gone before in Part III.

The scene is a cemetery near a chapel. A wizard enters, accompanied by a woman in mourning who expresses a wish to see the ghost of a certain man. She tells the wizard that this man appeared before her immediately after her wedding, stared at her wildly, but said not a word. The wizard (and the audience) is reminded of the speechless ghost whose apparition brought Part II to a close, and the wizard suggests that the ghost said nothing because it was the spirit of a living person. Such spirits "have no mouths."

Another wizard is celebrating the rites of Forefathers' Eve inside the chapel. Thousands of lights "like falling stars and fiery chains" glow round its roof; these are swarms of souls. Meanwhile, an apparition appears to the wizard, and we recognize the doctor of Scene VIII, his hands still scorched by the molten silver that caused his death. He is followed by a second ghost, who is being torn to pieces by black dogs. But neither of these specters is the man sought by the woman in mourning. As the cock crows thrice, she fears he will not attend the rites. To encourage her, the wizard utters an incantation, and they both behold "There, from the city of Wilno,/Amidst thick clouds of snow,/

A dozen carriages are flying,/All flying to the North." In the first of the carriages is a man in black, whom the woman instantly recognizes as the man she seeks: "He had one wound on his temples,/One only, and not large,/It seemed a black droplet." The wizard diagnoses this wound as a self-inflicted one that even Death cannot heal. But we may also inquire whether it indicates the wound that is perpetually renewed—that of human existence? In any case, the woman quietly beseeches God to heal him, and the act closes.

IV The Digression

What follows, in lieu of a second act or epilogue, is *The Digression,* a set of six long poems that follow the Polish exiles on their way into Russia, and that render in poetry Mickiewicz' own thoughts and feelings toward the problem of Russian-Polish relations. The visions, dreams, demons, and angels of Part III give way to a "real" world that is often ironically viewed by the poet.

Mickiewicz' attitude toward Russia was complex and underwent changes during his life. Up to the early 1820's, Lithuania—although partitioned along with the rest of Poland—was still administered to a certain extent by Poles; and there was little or no attempt at deliberate "Russification." During his youth in Wilno and Kowno, Mickiewicz and his contemporaries had not fully realized the dangers inherent in partition. Most Poles were still deluded into hoping that Tsar Alexander and his successor Tsar Nicholas were "angels of peace" who were well-intentioned toward Poland.

After his arrest, imprisonment, trial, and exile in 1823-24, Mickiewicz' attitude towards Russia underwent a fundamental and very natural change. He became politically mature, and his enforced stay of five years in Moscow, St. Petersburg, Odessa, and elsewhere as a political detainee gave him a profound insight into the tsarist system. But he continued to differentiate between the tsarist system and the Russian people, and he did not see any natural or elemental difference between Poles and Russians, who were all Slavs.

The 1830 Insurrection in Warsaw against the Russian occupation gave the Russian government an opportunity to incite hatred against Poland and the Poles in an attempt to increase unity within Russia itself. Now Mickiewicz began to see in the deliberate efforts made by the tsarist system to destroy Poland an immense symbol of the struggle between God and the Devil for the soul of his nation. This belief is expressed in *The Digression*, in which Mickiewicz appraises Russia through imagery. But the true interest of the work lies less in the concept, as stated in these general terms, than in the way Mickiewicz works it out in terms of poetry.

In the poem "The Road to Russia," the poet's "I" surveys the empty, apparently uninhabited territory "created as though yesterday" on which the deluges of history have left no mark, and which he sees as a blank sheet of paper waiting to be written upon. Later the traveler meets human beings who have massive bodies "like the animals and trees of the—North," but the face of each is like the country itself—"empty, open, ferocious." Their eyes are large and clear but lack any "spark of soul." The wilderness is crossed by roads "drawn by the finger of the Tsar from his capital," and along it travel black ranks of regiments despatched to fight at the tsar's command. Yet "None of them knows where he's going, or why?/None ask." The only other traffic on these roads is that of the sinister police carriages (*kibitki*). Their destination is unknown, and no one dares ask whom the carriages contain:

No doubt the Tsar has ordered someone to be seized.
"Perhaps the gendarme is coming from abroad?"
Says a general. "Who knows who has been trapped;
Perhaps the Prussian king, the King of France or Saxony?
Or some other German who's fallen from the Tsar's favor,
And the Tsar has decided to imprison him in a gaol?"

To his amazement, the general finally sees that the passengers are "young boys"; and, as the carriages fly past, he speculates they must be "the suspect children of some king or other."

The second poem, "Suburbs of the Capital," depicts St. Petersburg, the artificial creation of Peter the Great, erected early in the eighteenth century on a vast expanse of wasteland and marsh. Now rows of palaces rise along both sides of a magnificent avenue leading into the city:

> This looks like a church,
> With a dome, with a cross: there, like hay-ricks,
> Statues stand under the covering of straw and snow:
> Yonder, behind a row of Corinthian columns,
> Is a flat-roofed edifice, the Summer palace, in Italian style,
> Next are Japanese and Mandarin pagodas,
> Or freshly imitated Classical ruins
> From the Classical time of the Empress Catherine.

This jumble of incongruous styles and buildings rising on islands from the marshes was erected, like the circuses of pagan Rome, on "oceans of our blood and tears." The whole immense city, with its "two hundred thousand smoking chimneys," stands like a mirage in the desert. The chains worn by the Polish exiles are not removed, as "the prison gates are opened,/They search us, inquire, question—and let us in."

In the poem "Petersburg," the poet ironically contrasts the city with the other capital cities of Western civilization that were built as shrines of a divinity. But the origins of the Russian capital were different. It came into being in a barren land because the tsar willed a capital for himself, not for human beings: "Here the Tsar displayed the omnipotence of his will." He established the city on the bodies of a hundred thousand serfs by harnessing entire generations of his subjects to hard labor with wood and stones. In the next section of the poem, Mickiewicz reverts to his ironical tone: Peter the Great

> Recalled Paris—at once he ordered Parisian squares
> To be erected. He saw Amsterdam—
> Straightway he let the waters flow and put up dykes.
> He heard say there are great palaces in Rome—
> The palaces rise. The Venetian capital,
> Half on land and half in the water . . .
> Impresses the Tsar—and forthwith in his settlement
> He tore apart the marshy fields with canals.

But, though architects have a celebrated proverb to the effect that human hands built Rome and the gods built Venice, anyone who sees St. Petersburg cannot but say that it was surely built by demons.

We see the city next in terms of huge buildings of "marble on clay, clay on marble," all as regular as an army on parade. The visitor is bewildered by a babel of innumerable notices and advertisements: French lessons, sausage-maker, school for young ladies, ladies' dresses, sheet music, childrens' toys, or—the knout. In the streets no one stops, no one looks, no one speaks. This is the hour when the tsar is accustomed to walk abroad; so all society walks too—marshals, great ladies, officials—in straight rows, like playing-cards scattered by a card-sharper on both sides of the splendid avenue.

> But a few men were moving in this throng,
> Different from the rest by countenance and attire,
> They scarcely glance at the passers-by,
> But gaze at the city with stupefaction.
> They cast their gaze over the foundations,
> The walls, the towers, the iron and the granite,
> As if testing whether each brick is firmly placed:
> And they shrugged in despair,
> As if thinking: no man could overturn them!

Among them is a pilgrim; when the avenue empties, another figure appears, evidently an inhabitant of the city. The two men meet, and the latter reveals he too is a Pole. He greets the pilgrim with the sign of the Cross, but the pilgrim, preoccupied with his own thoughts, shuns the intruder. On the following day, however,

> when the confusion of his thoughts
> Slowly clears away and his memory grows fresh,
> He sometimes grieves for that intruder:
> If he meets him, he will recognize and stop him,
> Although he does not recall his countenance,
> Yet there was something in his voice and words
> Familiar to the pilgrim's ears and soul—
> Perhaps of him the pilgrim dreamed?

The fourth digression takes place in the poem "Monument of Peter the Great." This celebrated statue of the tsar on horseback is a symbol to Mickiewicz of the evil forces that helped build the terrible city. But, in front of it, "a pilgrim from the West, an unknown victim of the Tsar," meets "the bard of the Russian people," famed for his songs throughout the North. Mickiewicz does not identify this Russian poet, but he implies that he is a symbol of the creative imagination that transcends nationality. The Russian poet, who "quietly" comments on the monument to Peter, contrasts it negatively to the statue of Marcus Aurelius in Rome: "Not thus does the favorite of the people,/Marcus Aurelius stand forth in ancient Rome. . . ." The statue of Peter the Great, on the other hand, stands for tyranny: "A century he's stood, leaping without falling,/Like a waterfall flying out of granite rocks,/When, frozen into ice, it hangs over a precipice—". And he adds the cryptic question (to which no answer is forthcoming in the poem), "But when the sun of liberty will shine forth,/And a western wind warm these regions—/What then will become of the waterfall of tyranny?"

As Professor Lednicki has demonstrated, there is a close connection between this poem of Mickiewicz' and the celebrated *Bronze Horseman* of Pushkin (1833).[13] He suggests that the peculiar ambiguity to be found in Pushkin's great poem (which adds, of course, to its force) is due in part to its being an attempt at answering Mickiewicz' ironical and sardonic *Digression*. For all his good intentions, Pushkin was forced to imply the misery underlying the glories of St. Petersburg. Professor Lednicki has also shown that the image of St. Petersburg in Russian literature after 1833 is contaminated with much that is sinister, vile, and inhuman, as in the stories of Gogol and Dostoevsky (*Crime and Punishment* and later works), and including Andrei Biely's *Saint Petersburg* (1913).

The fifth and longest digression is "The Review of the Army," in which Mickiewicz describes and sardonically comments on the tsar's passion for military displays: "A coquette invited to a ball at the palace/Does not squander so much time before her mirror,/Does not make so many grimaces, blandishments,/As the Tsar every day on his parade-ground." The Imperial Dragoons, marching to the accompaniment of a "distant, monotonous, dull drum-beat," resemble rivers plunging into the parade ground as if it were a lake in which they lose what little identity they possessed as individuals. The heavy monotonous verse suggests a

terrible machine remorselessly sacrificing humanity, and it reveals implicitly the moral condition of Russian society under the
tsar. All the soldiers look alike:

> Like a line of horses chewing at the trough,
> Like hay-ricks tied into a sheaf,
> Like green flax in a field,
> Like the lines of a book, like the furrows of a field,
> Like the conversation in Petersburg drawing-rooms.

The hard clarity of these similes derives from the directness of
the poet's eye. They continue to multiply with ever-intensifying
ridicule: soon the countless soldiers resemble a spider with four
front and four back legs, then a tarantula or a fly. The entry of
the tsar with his entourage, glittering and gleaming like harle-
quins, is likened to a cloud of insects, in which "Each general is
a glowworm/Which glows beautifully on St. John's Eve;/But as
soon as the Springtime of the Tsar's favor passes,/The wretched
worms lose their brightness and sink into the mud they came
from."

The inhumanity of this society is made explicit when the parade
ground is deserted; only dead bodies of soldiers remain, frozen
to death during the maneuvers, or trampled underfoot, or beaten
to death by their officers.

The Digression concludes with "The Day before the Petersburg
Flood 1824: Oleszkiewicz." The individual named in the title is
a Pole greatly respected by Mickiewicz for his wisdom and virtue.
Two young travelers on the bank of the Neva at dusk see Oleszkiewicz brooding over the waters and prophesying in apocalyp-
tic language that the great flood about to descend upon the city
is a sign of Heavenly anger.

. . . . . .

We know from Mickiewicz' letters that *Forefathers' Eve* was
conceived and executed at white heat, and the metaphor is especially appropriate to this work because it conveys something of
the intensity of Mickiewicz' creative imagination and the striking
radiance of its result. No doubt Mickiewicz himself became more
precisely and vividly aware of the total experiences he projected

into the drama. We, however, can best respond to the meaning of this projected experience on two levels: on a level of conscious understanding and on an unconscious level of apprehension. On the second level, *Forefathers' Eve* in its entirety functions as myth, embodying the conflict of good and evil, which generates dramatic tension and which the poet has subjected to the elaborate, conscious, and sensitive control of art.

V Books of the Polish Nation and Pilgrimage

The "prophetic" vision of Father Peter in *Forefathers' Eve*, Part III, Scene V, his prophecy that the doctor will die at God's hand in Scene VIII, and the two parables by which he seeks to explain to the senator the meaning of his prophecies all find an echo in the *Books of the Polish Nation and Pilgrimage*. After completing *Forefathers' Eve*, probably *The Digression*, a number of shorter poems, and the translation of Byron's *Giaour*, Mickiewicz was obliged in 1832 to leave Dresden for Paris. He was not yet a political émigré but continued to travel on the Russian passport he had acquired when he left the country in 1829. He could have returned to Russia in a legal manner, but he declared in 1832: "I will never return to Russian rule, I have never, never had that intention."

When the Warsaw Insurrection against the Russian occupation broke out in November, 1830, Mickiewicz renounced his Russian passport as soon as the revolt was suppressed. He moved illegally to Paris, where the publication of *Forefathers' Eve*, Part III, was made possible in a printing house that had Polish type, and where lively publishing activity in Polish was already established.

Mickiewicz was by this time an important and widely admired figure in Polish literature, and his arrival in Paris was celebrated in Polish émigré circles. Already, too, he had attained the reputation of a model patriot; and he exerted extensive authority over his exiled contemporaries. His first manifesto addressed to these fellow-exiles was not poetry, as might have been expected, but the *Books of the Polish Nation and Pilgrimage*, published in December, 1832, at the same time as *Forefathers' Eve*, Part III. The book, or rather extended pamphlet, was produced in the shape of a prayerbook; and Mickiewicz had it distributed free of charge. In this respect Mickiewicz treated the work differently from his poetry, from which, after all, he had to make a living. Between April and June, 1833, he accepted the editorship of a small journal called *The Pilgrim*, for which he wrote a number of articles on current political topics, even though he was also working at this time on *Pan Tadeusz*.

The work is not primarily intended for readers of poetry, but Mickiewicz hoped to gain the widest possible distribution for his pamphlet among his contemporaries in exile. In it, he sought to propagate certain ideas of a religious and moral nature; and to achieve this end, he went back to the Bible and to the New Testament in particular. By associating his *Books* with Holy Writ, Mickiewicz deliberately tried to give the work the appearance of absolute, received wisdom.

Attitudes toward the Bible have undergone as many alterations during various literary periods as the attitude generally adopted by cultivated readers towards Shakespeare. In the Middle Ages, the Bible was the undisputed source of all wisdom; but, by the eighteenth century, discoveries in science—especially in geology and astronomy—had brought about a conflict between the theological and scientific viewpoints. The Bible gradually ceased to be regarded as a source of knowledge; it became instead a religious and moral treatise. The Romantics' attitude to the Bible was again different: with their cult of inspired poetry, of blended genres and styles, their admiration for what they considered "primitive" art, they turned to the Bible as the embodiment of prophetic poetry.

In a sense, *Books* is a "sacred parody" of one aspect of what is commonly called "the Biblical style" but without the humorous associations of that genre. The first sentence, characteristic of what was to follow, summarizes the work both in style and idea: "In the beginning was faith in one God, and there was freedom in the world." Here we are presented with a reminiscence of the Book of Genesis. Characteristic, too, is the total objectivity of the author himself: Mickiewicz does not explain his concept, or how he arrived at it. There is no framework of dream or vision to elucidate the statement; it is presented as though it were the Word.

Other aspects of so-called Biblical style that recur throughout *Books* are deliberate archaisms in vocabulary and syntax, the copious use of "And" to begin sentences, parallelisms (in which a series of phrases or sentences contain a number of the same elements, or are constructed in identical ways), and strongly rhythmic patterns that approach free verse. In addition, Mickiewicz uses parables and "commandments"; the former are marked by extreme simplicity and the elimination of details.

But *Books* is not merely a pastiche. The work is a poetic attempt to illuminate certain tendencies Mickiewicz has observed in the historical process. He adopts a religious and anti-rational attitude toward history as he presents not the creation of the universe, but a survey of the history of mankind. The religious and political doctrines in *Books* are closely linked with the mood prevailing among the Polish émigrés in the 1830's, shortly after the suppression and collapse of the Warsaw Insurrection. Mickiewicz takes as his main theme the brotherhood of nations, and he expresses his belief that the Polish pilgrims (or exiles) would very soon be required to take up arms again to ensure the revolutionary solidarity of the peoples of Europe. He stresses the need of preserving the patriotic unity of the émigrés, most of whom had passed through the fire of the Insurrection earlier that same year.

Much of *Books* is concerned with the moral betterment of the émigrés, for Mickiewicz considered this concern to be his own patriotic duty. Both Russian despotism and the Western European parliamentary system were hostile to the idea of the "liberation of the peoples," and especially of the Poles. A complete change in European political systems was essential. Nor was this all: *Books* also examines the contemporary state of religion and philosophy, with special reference to the work of Saint-Simon's ideas of a coming social Utopia.

Books contains few direct prophetic passages, but is imbued with a prophetic spirit. This aspect has long aroused critical controversy, and it may be responsible for the eclipse of Mickiewicz as a poet and artist that occurred during the nineteenth century. Regarded primarily as prophet and bard, he became the object of a mystical cult. *Books,* and Mickiewicz' later lectures in Paris in the 1840's (with which we shall not be concerned here), may be considered as the origins of the notion that Poland was the predestined martyr of the world. This idea was seized upon by later Romantic writers such as Krasiński and developed into a mystical belief known as Messianism, a doctrine both ill-defined and destructive to poetry (as Krasiński himself proved in *The Dawn* of 1843).

But the trouble with prophecy in literature is that it defeats its own purpose. Any prophetic writing is, by nature, selective; and it omits what is not in its own interest. As Chesterton said: "It is the nature of history to outwit its prophets." The popularity of such writing in the 1830's is not difficult to understand, however; like the prophetic writings of H. G. Wells, Aldous Huxley, George Orwell, and others in the 1930's, this popularity found its origin in a fear of the future and in a climate of anxiety. Mickiewicz, who was always highly sensitive to social and political trends, gave expression to this anxiety in his *Books*.

CHAPTER 6

Pan Tadeusz

*P*AN TADEUSZ (1834) is Mickiewicz' *Remembrance of Things Past*. From the harassments of subjectivity and the drama of self in *Forefathers' Eve* and from the realities of his predicament as a great poet in exile, deprived of an audience, Mickiewicz turned to discovering the collective life. He reveals a completely new aspect of his art, in which he displays a genuine interest in and an understanding of other people. No longer the Romantic prophet-bard endowed with mysterious powers that he has to express in dreams, visions, and nightmares, Mickiewicz now becomes the Romantic poet seeking to regain in art the ordered and stable world that has fallen apart. So Mickiewicz looks back to the Lithuania of the years 1811-12, when Polish society appeared to have achieved order, stability, and harmony—if only for a moment of time.

I *Need for Order*

Throughout *Pan Tadeusz* Mickiewicz dwells continually on the importance of order, ceremony, and ritual. His characters move within a precisely definable network of social relationships marked by courtesy, hospitality, respect, modesty, and patriotism; and every individual in this society has his proper place in the scheme of things. Yet this society was on the edge of a precipice into which it was destined—as Mickiewicz knew only too well— to vanish. Only the observance of law and morality, custom and convention could temporarily halt disaster. Mickiewicz was not interested in proving that these customs and conventions were right or wrong; he was very deeply concerned with the fact that they had existed in the past, and that this traditional way of life, although it had ceased to exist in time, was still alive in his own imagination.

So, moving onward from *Forefathers' Eve*, Mickiewicz turned to writing a "pastoral poem" along the lines of Goethe's *Hermann und Dorothea*. One of the classicist poets in the Warsaw drawing-room scene of *Forefathers' Eve* had commented on this literary genre: "We Slavs love the idyll." By putting the phrase into the mouth of one of his literary enemies, Mickiewicz clearly expressed his own attitude toward the idyll as a literary genre. He knew that the idyll and the pastoral had fallen into disrepute by the end of the eighteenth century, largely on account of its vapid and affected poetic diction; yet, only two years after making his derogatory comment, Mickiewicz began such a work.

As he knew, there is an essential difference between pastoral poetry and the idyll proper.[1] The two genres are related; but the idyll, which originated in Sicily long before the second century B.C., is of more ancient derivation. Among the isolated communities of Sicilian shepherds, a tradition was developed of holding contests of song between two or more individuals. The competitive nature of the tradition required the presence of a judge who becomes the third character. The subject of the shepherds' songs was customarily drawn from their own environment and experience: love, work, death, magic. The setting was rustic. All these elements contributed to the establishment of a formula that Theocritus adopted and developed, and writers to our own day have consciously drawn upon it. Pastoral poetry, on the other hand, is essentially descriptive and lacks the framework, structure, and organization that mark the idyll.

The Classical idyll found its way into Polish poetry in the seventeeth century with the *Idylls* of Simonides (1614). Writers of all successive literary movements and fashions used the form to produce idylls that accorded with their own taste: the Baroque idyll, the classical idyll, the sentimental idyll all made their appearance. Mickiewicz' *Pan Tadeusz* is the climax to these two centuries of development. But from its beginnings with the pastoral tradition, *Pan Tadeusz* extends its framework to epic length (twelve books), and becomes sufficiently expansive to incorporate anything Mickiewicz chooses—from comic and even farcical scenes to tragic incidents, character studies, observations of nature and things, satire, lyricism, and description. His only criterion was that everything should enhance, somehow, poetic truth.

Pan Tadeusz

II *Traditional Genre*

The title reads, in full: *Pan Tadeusz, or The Last Foray in Lithuania, A Tale of Gentlefolk in 1811 and 1812, in Twelve Books, in Verse.* A personal name as a title was, of course, traditional enough: Mickiewicz' own *Grazyna* and *Konrad Wallenrod* are in the same literary mode as Byron's *Don Juan* or *Childe Harold.* A subtitle was traditional, too, and it was only dropped when literary fashion changed. Mickiewicz' subtitle is traditional in that it explains what the poem is about. Even the word "tale" is traditional and occurred in Polish literature of the late Middle Ages in the *Tale of Rome, Tale of Troy,* and the like. By classifying the work as a "tale," Mickiewicz indicates that *Pan Tadeusz* is not an epic or a narrative poem, although it has genetic connections with these genres. *Pan Tadeusz* is, essentially, a characteristically Romantic work in the way it blends together a number of genres and exploits the individual qualities of each to achieve the poet's artistic purpose.

A significant word in the subtitle is the epithet "Last," which announces one of the poem's great themes—that of the past, the disappearance of tradition as exemplified in the "foray," or ritual execution of justice.

III *The Narrative*

The characters in *Pan Tadeusz* are presented with all the skill and insight of a great novelist, as well as with high poetic artistry. They fall into three intimately connected groups that are surrounded by a host of minor characters, and that are firmly established within a strongly visualized and localized setting. First Mickiewicz introduces Tadeusz himself—a rather susceptible young man just out of the university, who pays a visit in the summer of 1811 to the estate of his uncle, Judge Soplica, at Soplicowo. Within the next few days Tadeusz finds himself caught between two kinds of love for two different women: first for the innocent young girl Zosia; then for Zosia's guardian, Telimena, a worldly woman of a certain age, who has an eye for handsome young men and is visiting Soplicowo from St. Petersburg.

Parallel with the course of Tadeusz' sentimental entanglements (which Mickiewicz treats with humor and realism) is the "last foray" made against the Soplica estate by a count, a figure of high comedy. Urged on by an old manservant, the count attempts to regain possession of a ruined castle, which was formerly the property of his family but has now fallen by inheritance to the judge. The foray (Book VIII), despite its absurdity, has serious consequences in the lives of the characters.

The third group is centered round Father Robak, a Bernardine monk, whose history and even identity Mickiewicz (like a practiced story teller) keeps concealed until the climax of his plot. Minor characters include guests and officials in the judge's patriarchal household, impoverished Polish gentry in the neighborhood, the local Jewish innkeeper, and officers of the local Russian garrison.

The first ten books cover the events of five days and nights in 1811; the last two occupy a few hours during the summer of 1812. The action of *Pan Tadeusz* occurs, therefore, in two brief periods of time. But the five days and nights are not ordinary days and nights, since the personal fortunes and destinies of Tadeusz, Father Robak, the count, and Telimena all reach climaxes. In Books XI and XII, the fortunes of Poland and Lithuania are also depicted at a moment of crisis.

Book I. The Estate

Mickiewicz opens the poem with a celebrated invocation to Lithuania, which informs us that the poem is to deal largely with his own feelings and attitudes toward his homeland: "Today your beauty in all its glory/I can see and will describe, because I yearn for you." Despite this avowed intention, however, *Pan Tadeusz* is not a descriptive poem but the portrayal of human figures in a landscape. Mickiewicz establishes his authority for this undertaking by invoking the Virgin Mary, under whose protection lived the "faithful folk" of Lithuania and the poet himself as a child.

The action proper begins with the arrival of a young man at the Soplica manor house "years ago." He is not named as Tadeusz until line 168, but Mickiewicz indicates that he has the poet's sympathy; consequently, he wins ours. The gate of the manor house stands open, symbolizing the hospitality to be found within. Inside the house, with which Tadeusz has long been familiar, portraits of Polish national heroes indicate respect for tradition.

Tadeusz' susceptibilities are aroused almost at once by the sight of a girl in white, who vanishes before he can speak to her. Her white dress, her swan-like neck and shoulders—and other attributes of whiteness and light—have their traditional meaning of innocence and modesty. Her dress adumbrates the significance Mickiewicz places throughout his poem on the clothing worn by his protagonists. A character's dress indicates his or her nature; at the same time it expresses his or her place in the social order. The dress of the unknown, unnamed young girl is of the kind Lithuanian girls are accustomed to wear in the mornings, and in which they are not usually seen by men.

Judge Soplica welcomes Tadeusz and Mickiewicz takes the opportunity of this scene to emphasize the principles of order on which the household and estate are run. Other guests are strolling in the woods; soon they return

Gaily, but in order: first the little children
With their tutor: then the Judge and the Chamberlain's wife,
Next, the Chamberlain surrounded by his family,
The young ladies just behind their elders, the young men to one side,
The young ladies walking half a pace in front of the young men
(As decorum requires) : no one commented
On order, no one placed the company,
Yet each one involuntarily obeyed order.
For the Judge observed old customs in his home,
And never tolerated lack of respect
For age, birth, reason or rank.

(ll. 209-21)[2]

The judge is vexed to learn that his steward (Wojski) has had supper laid in the nearby ruined castle that is the object of dispute between the Soplica family and their neighbor, the count. However, the guests and members of the judge's extensive household enter the castle hall (again in proper order), and the meal begins with a traditional Lithuanian dish.

The supper is the first of several meals during the poem. Their symbolic nature is clear. These suppers, dinners, and banquets are not occasions for greed or gluttony; they are celebrated with all observances of rite and ceremony, subject to the proper order hallowed by tradition. The food and drink, themselves traditional, are often made according to special recipes (the *bigos*, IV, 964-85); served by special individuals entrusted with their preparation (the coffee, II, 491-510); eaten and drunk with special utensils (the centerpiece, XII, 33-169).

To Mickiewicz and his characters, the partaking of food and drink is an important function in the social order whose passing the poem celebrates. The meals are "ceremonies of love," [3] as they often are in the novels of Dickens. To partake of them demonstrates respect and affection for the other guests and for the host. Indeed, Mickiewicz clearly attaches a moral value to the ceremonial partaking of food and drink. The meals in *Pan Tadeusz* illustrate "wholesome appetite without greed, hospitality without ostentation, ceremony without pride or condescension." [4] Moreover, his loving enumeration of homely foods and rustic beverages contributes greatly to the strong sense of tangible reality that pervades the poem.

As the supper progresses, Mickiewicz, in his discreet role as the host in his own poem, introduces other guests who play parts in the story. There is the Bernardine monk, Father Robak, who looks askance at Captain Rykov, a Russian officer quartered in a nearby village. Rykov is a "good" Muscovite and claims to speak Polish, but his presence at the Soplica estate is a reminder that Lithuania was occupied by Russian troops in 1811. Once Robak and Rykov are established, Mickiewicz reverts to Tadeusz; and we see through his eyes the entrance to the supper table of Telimena, in pink silk, with lace, gloves and a gilded fan (ll. 538-48). Telimena is characterized at once by her inappropriate dress, which sets her apart from the rustic company and suggests affectation. Characteristically, too, Telimena does not partake of the supper. However, Tadeusz is impressed by her, although he is not yet twenty, and she is a woman of "mature years." They enter into a vivacious flirtation and within a half-hour are on intimate terms. In this episode, Mickiewicz introduces a variation on one of the great themes in *Pan Tadeusz*—the disparity between reality and illusion in human existence. Almost all the central characters in the poem are brought face to face with this disparity, and the ways they succeed or fail in coming to terms with it give the poem part of its meaning.

Pan Tadeusz

Meanwhile, at the other end of the supper table, the guests excitedly argue the virtues of their respective hunting dogs and arrange a rabbit hunt early next morning. When the supper is over, everyone leaves the table in proper order and retires to his bed. In one of the verbal jokes which occur from time to time in *Pan Tadeusz*, Mickiewicz depicts the judge's usher at his favorite bedtime reading: a Court Calendar, or list of names (ll. 878-83). This and other examples of Mickiewicz' virtuosity (I, 936-39; V, 861; VII, 85-90; XI, 316-18) display the complete mastery he has over all words—even personal names—enabling him to incorporate anything into his poetry.

Now follows one of Mickiewicz' ingenious transition passages that contribute to the inner coherence of the long poem:

Such were the diversions, arguments in those days
Amidst the quiet Lithuanian countryside: when the rest of the world
Drowned in tears and blood, when a man, the God of War,
Surrounded by a storm-cloud of regiments, thousands of cannons,
Had harnessed to his chariot gold and silver eagles,
And was flying from the Libyan desert to the lofty Alps
Hurling thunderbolts . . .

Despite the isolation of the Soplicowo manor, the judge and his neighbors are kept informed of the events abroad by wandering beggars and also by Father Robak, the monk. When all the guests are asleep, Robak seeks out the judge, for whom he has news. But Mickiewicz exercises his prerogative as the poem's host to conceal from us what the news may be, and in doing so he suddenly intensifies the air of mystery surrounding the monk.

Book II. The Castle

As the guests at Soplicowo set off hunting early next morning, the poet again turns his observant eye and ear upon the remembered landscape:

There a corn-crake shrieks from the meadow, seek him in vain,
He'll skim through the grass like a pike in the Niemen;
There overhead the early bell of Spring resounds,
A lark concealed deep in the sky;
Yonder an eagle's wide wings rustled,

Scaring the sparrows like a comet scared the Tsar,
While a hawk, suspended in the clear firmament
Flutters his wings like an impaled butterfly
Until, discerning a bird or rabbit in the grass,
He plunges upon it from above like a falling star.

Even though their prey is merely rabbit, the hunting party observe order and decorum. As soon as they are out of sight, Count Horeszko makes his first appearance. Like Telimena, he is distinguished by his inappropriate and un-Polish attire: a long white frock coat of English cut, its tails flying in the wind. His servants, whom he calls "jockeys," wear "little shiny black hats like mushrooms," short jackets, top boots, and white pantaloons. As the count gazes at the castle ruins looming in the early morning mist, Mickiewicz comments, "The Count loved unusual, new sights,/He called them romantic: he used to say he had/A romantic mind: in fact, he was a great eccentric." The count, even more than Tadeusz, is to be a victim of the illusion-reality disparity.

He catches sight of old Gervazy, the last of the Horeszko family retainers, suitably attired in Horeszko livery—a yellow tail-coat and epaulettes "once gold but now faded to yellow." The count mentions to the old man that he has tired of the expensive and protracted litigation he and the judge have been engaged in over possession of the castle and is prepared to resign his claim. Dismayed, Gervazy warns his master there can be no agreement between the Horeszko and Soplica families, for two decades earlier, during the Kościuszko rebellion of 1794, Jacek Soplica, brother of the judge, killed a Horeszko and fled the country. No one knows what became of him.

The romantically-minded count is delighted by this tale, which recalls the legends of bloody deeds committed in the castles of English and Scottish lords. His honor is at stake, and he decides after all to break off the negotiations with Judge Soplica. Once his decision is made, the count sets off to join the hunt. Then

> in a moment of forgetfulness
> He glanced around and reigned his horse by a fence;
> There was a garden.
> Fruit trees standing in rows,
> Overshadowed a wide field: beneath them, vegetables.

> Here sits a cabbage, bowing his venerable bald head,
> And seems to ponder the fate of vegetables;
> There, twining his pods in the green hair of carrots,
> A slender bean turns myriad eyes upon her:
> Yonder rise the golden tassels of maize,
> Elsewhere, see the belly of a stout pumpkin
> Who has wandered from its parent stem
> To visit with the crimson beets.

In this celebrated comic passage, Mickiewicz has endowed nature and the vegetable world with human traits and with the potentialities of feeling that human beings possess. By likening nature to people, and sometimes people to nature, Mickiewicz throughout the poem implies the close relationships existing between his characters and their surroundings. His imagined universe is one of unity, order, and harmony.

The count perceives in this garden a girl in white, wearing a straw hat, gathering fruit. He gazes "with neck outstretched, like a long-billed/Crane, far from its flock, as it stands in wait/On one leg, with watchful eyes, holding a stone/In the other foot, lest it fall asleep." He is aroused from his contemplation by Father Robak, who has a way of appearing at inopportune moments, and who warns the count that the fruit in this garden is not for him. When he looks again, the girl has vanished.

The hunting party has returned to the manor for breakfast, a meal at which less formality and fewer conventions than usual are observed, somewhat to the judge's disapproval. Coffee is served, and Mickiewicz comments, "Such coffee as in Poland is not to be had elsewhere;/In Poland, in a respectable home, by ancient custom,/There's a particular woman charged with coffee-making,/Called the coffee-maker." Mickiewicz fondly enumerates the ingredients and method used to prepare and drink the beverage.

During breakfast, the count is discussed. Despite an invitation he did not join the hunting party; we learn that he was brought up abroad and holds the view that "civilisation is greater among the Muscovites" than in Poland because there hunting is strictly regulated by the tsar's laws and enforced by police. Telimena protests that the count is right, adding, "I know Russia well. No one here believes me/When I've sometimes said how admirable is the vigilance and severity of its laws." She launches into a prolonged and uncritical monologue in praise of St. Petersburg where she lives, boasts of her fashionable acquaintances, and exposes herself as absurdly affected—one of the *grandes coquettes* satirized on the contemporary Russian stage by playwrights such as Shakhovskoi and Zagoskin.[5] Yet, such is Mickiewicz' understanding of and affection for all his characters, including Telimena, that her self-portrait is not a caricature but a comic creation of the highest order.

Book II ends with Telimena, bored by the others' conversation, leading the whole company out to gather mushrooms in the woods.

Book III. Flirtation

On his way home, the count keeps stopping his horse to look back at the vegetable garden. Unable to contain his curiosity about the girl, he dismisses his servants and creeps stealthily into the garden "like a wolf entering a stable." In the brilliantly colored scene of almost farcical comedy that follows, he encounters a goose-girl whom, true to his Romantic illusions, the count takes for a hapless heroine kept prisoner by a cruel guardian. He offers to rescue her; but the girl, diverted by his poetic outburst, asks him kindly to drive her poultry back from the cornfield: "The charm, the magic, the miracle,—are over." A chain of psychological reactions sets in; at first the disillusioned count continues to stand alone in the garden, "His soul, like the earth at sunset/ Slowly grew cold, took on darker hues." Gradually his mind begins to function again, and he pulls his hat down over his head and begins worrying lest anyone observed his discomfiture. Looking cautiously around, he is the spectator of a mysterious scene:

> Under a tent of drooping green branches,
> A multitude of shapes was wandering, with strange gestures,
> As if dancing, their strange attire made them look like spirits
> Wandering on the moon. Some in tight black,
> Others in long, sweeping robes, bright as snow . . .
> All continually leaned in various directions,
> Down to the ground, as if curtseying.
> If they approach or meet together
> They neither speak nor greet each other.

The count instantly takes them for the shades who dwell in the Elysian fields, but Mickiewicz knows better: "Who'd have guessed that those almost motionless,/Those silent people—are our friends,/The Judge's company! From the talkative breakfast/ They've come to the solemn rite of mushroom-gathering." As always in *Pan Tadeusz*, everyone throws himself wholeheartedly into whatever he may be doing—whether it is hunting, eating, or mushrooming. Mickiewicz takes the opportunity to digress into another display of linguistic virtuosity as he catalogues the various species of mushroom to be found in Lithuania: the fox-mushroom, the pine-lover, the orange-agaric, the fly-bane, leaf-mushrooms, puff-balls, and "whites". (ll. 260-289).

But Telimena is already bored with the mushrooming and wanders away to a wooded hillock, which she calls her Temple of Meditation. Here she strikes an interesting pose:

> On the thick emerald grass, in a cornelian shawl,
> A long gown, as though enveloped in coral,
> From which at one end gleamed her hair,
> And from the other her black shoes: gleaming,
> Her snow-white stockings, handkerchief, white hands and countenance,
> She seemed from a distance a multi-colored caterpillar,
> Which creeps along a green maple-leaf.

Here Telimena is joined by the judge, who has already noticed his nephew Tadeusz' sentimental interest in her, and who takes it upon himself as the boy's guardian to discuss his future. He mentions in passing that Tadeusz' father, Jacek Soplica, is living abroad, and for some reason best known to himself prefers not to let Tadeusz know he is still alive. Mickiewicz sets and develops this scene with all the skill of a practised novelist. The dialogue serves at least two purposes: first, Telimena reveals new facets of her character as she speaks feverishly, with copious exclamations and interruptions; the judge, in contrast, uses simple, clear, and logical arguments. Second, the dialogue provides us with certain items of information essential to our understanding of the story that is unfolding.

When the judge has made his point, he leaves Telimena still in a state of some agitation. Almost at once both Tadeusz himself and the count converge upon Telimena in her temple. They are rivals for her favor, and, as is appropriate in this rural setting, Mickiewicz has the two young swains embark upon a poetic contest. They debate the relative beauties of Italian and Lithuanian landscapes (ll. 492-681). The contest is interrupted by the distant dinner bell recalling the mushroom gatherers to the manor; Telimena rewards the count with a forget-me-not, but the real prize goes to Tadeusz, as she furtively slips him a door key wrapped up in a note.

At dinner, the judge's forester announces that a bear has been seen in the forest; this is the signal for the company to resolve on a bear hunt the next day.

Book IV. Diplomacy and Hunting

Mickiewicz now penetrates, in his imagination, into the immemorial forests of Lithuania with all their historical associations and personal recollections. In the forest heart "It is terrible to glance: there sit the lords of the forest,/Wild boars, bears, wolves: at the gateway lie bones/Of half-devoured and unwary guests." The forest is also inhabited by stags, woodpeckers, and the squirrel

> holding a nut in her paws,
> She bites it; her bushy tail waves over her head
> Like the plume on a helmet of a cuirassier;
> Although thus sheltered, she glances round;
> Sees an intruder, leaps like a forest dancer
> From tree to tree, flashes like lightning,
> Finally she plunges into the hidden opening of a stump,
> Like a dryad returning to her native tree.

At Soplicowo, Tadeusz is still snoring despite the noisy preparations for the bear hunt. A tap on the shutter awakes him:

> his wakening was joyful,
> He felt lively as a bird, breathed quicker,
> Was happy, smiled to himself,
> Thinking of what had happened yesterday
> He blushed and sighed and his heart throbbed.

Has Tadeusz used the door key with which Telimena rewarded him? Mickiewicz discreetly declines to say. When he jumps out of bed, Tadeusz catches sight of two bright eyes peeping through the heart-shaped aperture in the shutter. As before, however, the girl vanishes before he can throw the shutter open and address her. Hastily he follows the hunting party to where "Two taverns lean on either side the road,/Their windows threatening each other like enemies,/The old tavern belongs by law to the castle,/The other Soplica erected to spite the castle." Mickiewicz provides a long and elaborate description of the older tavern which from a distance resembles "a Jew bowing down to pray,/The roof's his hat, the tousled thatch his beard,/The smokey dirty walls his black robe,/The carved facade projects like buttons on his brow." The tavernkeeper is Jankiel, an old Jew well known for his honesty, a model citizen and patriot with a fondness for music, which he puts to excellent use later in the poem. Local gossip declares that Jankiel is in league with Father Robak, and that Robak is engaged in smuggling. Mickiewicz hastens to deny this, though the gossip is at least partly true: what Robak is smuggling into Russian-occupied Lithuania, however, is not goods but ideas.

Robak is inside the tavern with a crowd of local gentry, and Mickiewicz depicts the priest's skill in dominating and impressing the minds of his simple audience, not by preaching, but by anecdotes and symbolic names, including that of Napoleon. Catching sight of Tadeusz galloping past the tavern, Robak hastens to follow him. They both ride into the forest, and the bear hunt begins (ll. 566-659). At this point, Mickiewicz increases the pace of his narrative: the rapidity of action is marked by short, simple phrases, sometimes broken by or interspersed with cries and exclamations from the hunters.

The bear is sighted, and "within the forest depths is heard a roar,/Then from the undergrowth, as if out of a cloud, the bear rushed like a thunderbolt:/Around him the hounds pursuing, leaping, howling: he has risen on his hind legs,/And glances around, terrifying his foes by roaring." Tadeusz and the count find themselves directly in his path; but before the bear can attack them, three shots are heard simultaneously: "The bear leaped up like a hare at hounds,/His head fell back, his four paws/Went head over heels, his weight of bloody body/Fell upon the Count and knocked him off his feet. . . ." The death of the bear is the signal for the steward to seize his hunting horn, which

> like a tempest of eloquent air
> Raises music in the forest and echo resounds.
> The hunters fell silent, the beaters stood amazed
> By the force, purity and strange harmony of the sound.
> The old man displayed the art he'd once been famed for,
> Once again to the ears of the hunters,
> Filling and enlivening the groves and thickets.

The bear's death is celebrated by a hunt breakfast held in the open air, and Book IV ends with a series of comic genre scenes.

Book V. The Brawl

The bear hunt over, another hunt begins—Telimena, alone in the manor house, wonders how she can entrap Tadeusz and the count. We overhear her thoughts in an "inner monologue":

> The Count's a young nobleman,
> Heir to a great name, attractive, charming;
> Already a trifle in love! What if he be fickle?
> And again—is he sincere? Does he want to marry
> A woman a few years older—and not wealthy?
> Will his relatives agree? What would the world say?

Tadeusz, on the other hand, is "a simpleton, an honest lad!/ Almost a child still. Just beginning to fall in love for the first time." Telimena wonders whether a practical solution to her dilemma would be to marry off the count to her ward, Zosia.

Now, for the first time, Mickiewicz presents the poem's heroine in person; hitherto she has been an ethereal presence observed by Tadeusz or the count in the very act of disappearing. Zosia is feeding poultry

> rough-feathered hens
> Trundle up in clouds, crested roosters
> Flourishing red combs on their heads

> Rowing with their wings over furrows and stubble,
> Stretching out their long-spurred feet,
> Behind them moves a puffed-up turkey,
> Complaining at the gobble of his noisy spouse.

Telimena is shocked to find her ward at this pastime and decides the time has come to bring her out into society. The transformation of Zosia from a country miss into a young lady of fashion is now effected by the ceremonial of dressing (ll. 145-168), which ends as the hunting party returns from the forest. Telimena formally introduces Zosia to Tadeusz: "But he, on glancing into Zosia's eyes, grew so agitated/That, standing dumb before her, first he blushed, then paled:/What was in his heart even he himself did not divine." Telimena watches him intently all the time. Vexed and jealous, she begins to reproach him until Tadeusz, losing his temper, leaves the room with a slam of the door. Fortunately none of the other guests notice this scene.

Tadeusz wanders disconsolately about the countryside until he comes to the Temple of Meditation which, yesterday, had been a witness of his happiness. Telimena is already there, and she is in tears. As Tadeusz is about to approach her, she

> suddenly jumps up from her seat,
> Rushes right, then left, jumps across the little stream,
> Arms outstretched, hair loose, pale,
> She dashes into the wood, jumps, kneels, falls,
> Unable to rise, she crouches on the turf,
> From her gestures plainly she is in terrible agony.

Alarmed, Tadeusz seeks to help her—only to discover that the cause of her extraordinary behavior is that she had inadvertently been sitting too close to an ant hill. As they brush away the insects, a tender reconciliation is effected, lasting until they hear the dinner bell.

After the guests have made their customary formal entry into the castle ruin, where the meal is to be served, Mickiewicz invites us to contrast this meal with the supper of Book I. Now the mood of his characters has grown somber. Tadeusz is jealous of the count, who is talking to Zosia; and he also observes that Telimena's complexion is not as fine as he thought—some of her powder and rouge have come off, revealing wrinkles. Telimena in turn fears the count may have observed her in the Temple of Meditation with Tadeusz. The count is reminded of his claim to possession of the castle and grows sulky. The assessor and the regent, two officials in the judge's household, continue an argument they began in Book I. Gradually the atmosphere worsens until the count, provoked, threatens the judge and, after an unseemly brawl, is literally thrown out of the supper room. He and old Gervazy decide the time has come to seize the castle by force.

Book VI. The Hamlet

The changed mood and tone of the dinner scene persists into the following day (the fourth), which opens ominously with mist, rain, and silence. Gradually, however, the landscape grows populated: "On the highroad and byways from early morning/Unusual traffic has prevailed." Peasant carts, gentlefolk's carriages, and messengers drive hither and thither. Interested but alarmed, the judge's comptroller hastens to inform his master, whom he finds in the act of writing out a formal charge against the count for his insulting behavior on the previous day.

In an extended scene (ll. 102-296) consisting for the most part of dialogue, Father Robak attempts to dissuade the judge from proceeding with his charges. Reconciliation is all the more necessary now because, as Robak reminds the judge,

> War is impending,
> A war for Poland! Brother! We shall be Poles again!
> War is certain! When I made my way here on a secret
> mission,
> The army's vanguard was already on the Niemen;
> Napoleon is gathering a vast army,
> Such as no man ever saw, nor history recalls:
> Beside the French a whole Polish army is on the march,
> Our Joseph Poniatowski, our white eagles!
> They are on the way, at Napoleon's first signal,
> They will cross the Niemen and our homeland will be
> resurrected.

For all his hopes, the judge is stubborn and refuses to take the first step toward any reconciliation with the count.

Meanwhile the judge's usher has reached the count's house for the purpose of delivering the charge. To his surprise the house is deserted except for two old women, who inform him that the count and his servants have all set off, armed, to the hamlet of Dobrzyn. Mickiewicz introduces the Dobrzynski family, who inhabit the hamlet. Once powerful and wealthy, the family has now come down in the world, and "they are forced to work for themselves,/Like hired serfs! but russet smocks/They will not wear, only black and white striped coats,/And frock coats on Sunday." As elsewhere in *Pan Tadeusz*, clothing is an important factor in the elaborate scheme of order Mickiewicz is imaginatively reconstructing. Despite their poverty, the Dobrzynski family cling to the outward signs of their gentility, though financially they are little better off than the peasants.

The hamlet consists of a tavern, a church, and the Dobrzynski farmstead. Evidence of age and decay is everywhere: the roof is overgrown with moss and grass, birds nest in the attics and windows, rabbits hop to and fro on the threshold.

> Yet once the house had been fortified. Everywhere
> Were signs it had undergone great and frequent attacks.
> Even now, by the gate, like a baby's head
> A huge cannon-ball lay in the grass,
> Memento of the Swedish wars.

The Dobrzyn hamlet serves as an emblem of the entire Polish state, in decline from its period of greatness.

Neighboring gentry have gathered at the hamlet in response to a call to arms by the count's old retainer, Gervazy. The head of the Dobrzynski family, Maciej, welcomes them, and they prepare to discuss what should be done. Book VII, *The Council*, presents the course of the debate, during which Gervazy tries to inflame the gentry against the judge. The principal speakers are Bartek the Prussian—so called because he detests Prussians; Maciej the Baptist; the "politician" Buchman; and Jankiel, the tavern-keeper. The count himself, wearing a "brown cloak of Italian cut" and a feathered hat, and followed by ten armed "jockeys," rides into the hamlet, to be greeted by the assembly. All proceed to the tavern for a libation (ll. 530-9); then they set off toward Soplicowo with the cry "Down with the Soplicas!"

Book VIII. The Foray

The calm that heralds a storm is expressed in the opening paragraphs of Book VIII:

> After supper, the Judge and his guests from the manor
> Go out into the courtyard to enjoy the evening;
> They sit themselves down on moss-strewn benches,
> The entire group gloomily and silently
> Gaze at the sky, which seems to lower,
> To press down and lie ever closer to the earth.

They listen to the "strange music of evening":

> The owl began it, hooting on the manor roof;
> Bats whispered on brittle wings, they flit
> Round the house where windowpanes and human faces gleam;
> Closer still, the little sisters of bats,
> Moths swarm and hover, drawn by the ladies' dresses.

Further off, in the fields, the concert has only just begun:

> The musicians finish tuning their instruments,
> Three times the corn-crake shrieks, the meadows' first fiddler,
> The bitterns boom an answer to him from the marsh,
> Woodcocks in their rising flight
> Beat with their wings like tiny drums.

In an attempt to dispel the gloomy atmosphere surrounding the party, the judge's usher delivers a lecture on the stars and relates legends associated with them (ll. 61-104). Meanwhile the judge himself calmly awaits the return of Father Robak, convinced the latter will have been able to pacify the count. When the other guests retire, Tadeusz decides to seek out his uncle and ask his advice; but the judge's door is locked, for he is engaged in secret discourse with Robak. Hearing sobs within, Tadeusz ventures to peep through the keyhole and sees "a strange sight." The judge and Father Robak, both in tears, are kneeling and embracing. Robak confesses he has been living as a Bernardine monk "in the service of God and my homeland," and had hoped to keep his true identity secret even from the judge and "his own son." But Maciej Dobrzynski has recognized him, and he fears this discovery will lead to the undoing of the conspiracy for which he works.

Tadeusz, who is too preoccupied with his own problems to ponder the significance of this brief scene, waits for Robak to leave and then enters the judge's chamber. The plot line takes on an entirely new and unexpected direction as Tadeusz tells his uncle he has resolved to quit Soplicowo and to join the Polish army with Napoleon's forces, who are preparing to invade Russia. Before he goes, however, he will challenge the count to a duel. At first, the judge does not take Tadeusz seriously; then he begins to suspect him of trifling with the feelings of Zosia. Finally, he angrily informs Tadeusz he must marry the girl or be disinherited.

Pondering as he leaves his uncle's room, Tadeusz suddenly comes face to face with a ghost: "All in white, tall, slender, emaciated,/It glided towards him with outstretched hand/On which the trembling moonlight gleamed." The ghost speaks to him first (this proves it is not a "real" one): "Oh, ungrateful one!/Formerly you sought my gaze, now you avoid it,/You sought converse with me, today you refuse to listen/As though there were venom in my words and looks." Tadeusz recognizes Telimena, and in the dialogue that follows she rings all the changes on a woman scorned—from theatrical and bitter outbursts of laughter to sobs of despair. She tries to cajole him, then accuses herself; when neither method prevails over Tadeusz, Telimena descends to sarcasm, and when that too is of no avail, she turns on him in fury and calls him "liar." Throughout her tirades, Tadeusz has behaved like a gentleman; but this insult is unpardonable: "Tadeusz shuddered, his face turned pale as a corpse,/He stamped his foot, bit his lip, said: 'And you're a fool.'" Leaving her, Tadeusz has to argue with his conscience and decides that the only solution to his dilemma is to do away with himself. He reaches the lake, and there meets the count followed by his troop of jockeys. The count takes Tadeusz prisoner (and thus prevents him from suicide, which, however, Mickiewicz never let us take seriously). They proceed to the Soplicowo manor and capture the judge, the ladies, and the rest of the household. By the time the Dobrzynskis and their allied gentry arrive with Gervazy, all is over. Soplicowo is in the hands of the count and his followers, and there is nothing left for the rural gentry to do but celebrate the victory by looting the cellar and pantries.

Book IX.   The Battle

So soundly do the count's supporters sleep that "they are not aroused/By the gleam of lanterns and entry of a dozen men,/ Who fell upon the gentry like wall-spiders." The simile reveals Mickiewicz' attitude towards the intruders, who are Russians from the nearby garrison. By the time the judge's allies arrive to take his side, the Russians have put the count and his jockeys under guard and have thrown the gentry into improvised stocks where they "Sat in a row, their teeth chattering with cold,/Out in the rain, for the downpour has increased." The sun rises blood-red on the scene, a wind rises, driving thick and ragged clouds out of the east.

The Russian detachment is under the command of Major Plut, a Russianized Pole and renegade, "a great rascal, as usually happens/With a Pole who becomes a Muscovite in the Tsar's service." Plut's coarse and cynical attitude, and finally his drunken attempt to kiss Telimena, lead Tadeusz to slap Plut in the face and challenge him to a duel. The ensuing uproar leads to an extended battle between the Poles, who are now united against their enemies, the Russians. The course of the battle is described in a rapid series of brief scenes between individuals. Despite the arrival of Russian reinforcements, and their more up-to-date weapons (rifles with bayonets), the Poles eventually gain the upper hand. The climax comes when a large outhouse, used for storing cheeses, is overturned upon the heads of the Russians. Those who are not killed are routed by the gentry, and as the Book ends: "Plut was long sought for: he, in a clump of nettles,/Deeply concealed, lay as if dead:/Finally he emerged on seeing the battle was over." He disappears from the poem, and Mickiewicz informs us (ll. 199-204) that he was never heard of again. Thus ended the last foray in Lithuania.

Book X.   Emigration—Jacek Soplica

The storm which rose early in the morning of the Soplicowo battle dies down momentarily:

> And there was a time of quietude: and the wind stood
> Mute, silent, as if speechless with terror.
> And the cornfields which earlier bowed to the ground
> Or, shaking their golden ears,
> Ebullient as waves, now stand motionless . . .

Then the winds suddenly rise again, and a downpour begins:

> Now the earth and sky are covered quite,
> Night darkens them with a storm darker than night.
> Sometimes the horizon cracks apart from end to end,
> And the angel of storms, in the shape of an immense sun,
> Reveals his face . . .

Although the Poles have temporarily defeated their oppressors, the position is dangerous; and they expect reprisals. Fortunately the storm cuts Soplicowo off from the world and provides a little time for them to consider what must be done. The warden (Podkomorzy), a highly respected neighbour of the judge, urges the younger men to flee the country.

Tadeusz, who has become engaged to Zosia at his uncle's instructions, is obliged to bid her farewell. Seeing this, the count bids an eloquent farewell to Telimena; but Mickiewicz' ironical tone and the language he puts into the mouths of the count and Telimena reassure us that they are both merely posing.

Tadeusz leaves before Father Robak can reveal his identity and his relationship to the young man. The priest, whose earlier wounds are troubling him, has been forced to take to his bed. Predicting his own death, Robak sends for a priest; and in another extended scene, Robak makes his confession. We learn that he was Jacek Soplica, and that he fled abroad after the murder of the head of the Horeszko family. During exile, he was "transformed" by the grace of God into the humble monk Robak. As he lies dying, his main concern is to obtain the forgiveness of old Gervazy, the last surviving retainer of the Horeszko family, who witnessed the murder.

Before Robak breathes his last, the tavernkeeper Jankiel hastily rides up to the manor with a letter for the monk. The letter is from Fiszer, Chief of Staff of the Polish army; and it announces

that Napoleon's cabinet has decided to declare war, that a Sejm
has been convoked in Warsaw, and that the Confederate States of
Mazovia have solemnly vowed to liberate Lithuania. All kneel,
and in a final tableau Mickiewicz presents the apotheosis of Father Robak:

> The night was just departing and across the milky sky
> The first pink sun-rays hasten;
> They fell through the windowpanes like diamond arrows,
> They gleamed around the head of the dying man
> And invested his brow and countenance with gold,
> So that he shone like a saint in a fiery crown.

Book XI. The Year 1812

The route of Napoleon's Grand Army, which includes Polish
battalions under General Dabrowski, leads them through Lithuania toward Moscow. As the armies pass near Soplicowo, the judge
prepares to welcome the Polish troops with a ceremonial banquet.
The great day arrives, and "the people of Lithuania from the
entire neighbourhood/Have gathered at dawn around the chapel,/
As if for the revelation of a new miracle." After the celebration of
Mass, the warden appears in the resplendent attire of a Palatine
and delivers a stately eulogy in honor of the late Father Robak.

Among the Polish officers is Tadeusz, in the uniform of a
Lancer, his right arm in a sling ("evidently he has been
wounded"). He is no longer the susceptible simpleton of the previous year, but has acquired feelings of responsibility and duty,
which he expresses to Zosia:

> You must tell me,
> Before we exchange rings, I must know it—
> What of it that last year you were ready
> To be my betrothed? Then I did not accept it,
> What to me was a promise given under force?

Zosia reassures him in a brief, unaffected confession of love. All go
into the great hall of the castle to await the banquet: Zosia, in a
simple, harmoniously colored Lithuanian dress, is the center of
attention. Among the guests is the count, "Not long a soldier, but
since he had a great fortune/And raised at his own expense an

entire regiment of cavalry,/And had conducted himself courage-
ously in his first battle,/The Emperor had this very day promoted
him to colonel." The action of Book XII, *Let Us Love One Another!*, follows immediately on that of Book XI; and Mickiewicz
indicates this by linking them with a rhyme. The last Old Polish
banquet begins; and its importance is symbolized by the use of a
splendid centerpiece adorned with figures in Polish costume,
which has long historical associations with the judge's family. As
the banquet proceeds, the centerpiece changes color from sugared
ice to green and then to gold; and the guests begin to partake of
it with their wine.

The count and Telimena meet again. She is engaged to marry
the judge's notary, and the count seizes this opportunity to in-
dulge in a theatrical scene: "'Is it you?' he cried, 'do my eyes deceive me?/ 'You—in my presence? You press another's hand!/'O,
faithless being, O changeable soul!/ 'And yet you do not sink into
the ground for shame?'" In contrast to the posing and affectation of
the count and Telimena, Tadeusz and Zosia are united in a vision
of love that Tadeusz celebrates by deciding to liberate the serfs.
The serfs, gathered in the courtyard, greet this news with enthusiasm; and Jankiel, the tavernkeeper, is persuaded to play upon
his dulcimer. Jankiel's concert symbolizes, in music, events in
Polish history; and it is followed by a polonaise, in which the
entire company takes part:

> And they proceeded pair by pair, noisily and gaily,
> The circle turned and twisted like a huge snake,
> Breaking into a thousand convolutions;
> The variegated, colored costumes change,
> Ladies, lords, officers, like glistening scales
> Gilded by the beams of the westering sun.

The symbolic meaning of this stately, traditional Polish dance,
which brings *Pan Tadeusz* to its close, has caught the imagination
of Polish writers. In the last scene of Stanislaw Wyspianski's *The
Wedding* (1900), the final polonaise danced by all the characters
means the restoration of order after the supernatural events that
went before. In Jerzy Andrzejewski's novel *Ashes and Diamond*
(1948), the polonaise is still closer in meaning to that of *Pan
Tadeusz* and stands directly for the passing away of the old order.

In a final couplet, Mickiewicz affirms again the truth of his poem: "And I too was a guest there, I drank mead and wine,/ What I saw and heard I have contained in these books."

IV *Objectivity and Realism*

This summary and the paraphrases have perforce omitted that which makes *Pan Tadeusz* what it is—namely, the poetry. Translation cannot begin to convey the total effect of the poem, which emerges from the close interaction of style, diction, and word associations with the portrayal of characters, the presentation of setting, and the evocation of a powerfully felt atmosphere.

Nevertheless, other features of the poem which contribute to its total effect and meaning can be perceived through the medium of paraphrase. They include Mickiewicz' treatment of his two main themes: the recapture of the past and the conflict between reality and appearance in human life. These are two of the most enduring themes in Western literature, and Mickiewicz' handling of them in *Pan Tadeusz* endows the poem with universal reference, despite the writer's identification with a unique cultural and historical tradition and the poem's unfamiliar setting.

Looking back to his childhood, Mickiewicz sought—like Proust —to confer life on a society that had ceased to exist nearly two decades earlier. He could only achieve this task through art. Fortunately Mickiewicz throughout his career as a writer possessed the rare quality of mind best described as critical intelligence. Thanks to this quality, he escaped the notorious Romantic malady that afflicted many of his contemporaries and has brought their work into disrepute.

One consequence of the exercise of the critical intellect on the poetic material of *Pan Tadeusz* was that Mickiewicz achieved the objectivity his themes called for. In order to embody these themes most effectively in poetry, Mickiewicz had to depict them in terms of individuals in society; and, for vivid and clear characterization all writers need a measure of objectivity. For this reason Mickiewicz' characters speak for themselves in the poem—in action as well as in words. Almost half the poem is cast in the form of dialogue. Mickiewicz is standing aside to allow his protagonists to act out their lives before us in the dramatic present. This method of proceeding is exemplified in the capital scene between

Tadeusz and the jealous Telimena, which immediately follows a strongly visualised scene between Tadeusz and the judge (Book VIII). Mickiewicz does not tell us what his characters feel, but reveals their states of mind principally by what they say, and also by means of exterior manifestations (gestures, looks, reactions). During the course of this scene, Telimena's varying emotions are expressed in her own words and by her behavior: she replies "with a bitter smile," she "bursts into tears," "begins to sob," and "falls upon Tadeusz' neck." When Tadeusz seeks to leave her, she "stopped with an eye/And face like the Gorgon's head: he had to remain/Despite himself: he gazed in alarm at her countenance,/ She stood pale, motionless, deprived of breath, of life!" Her utterances grow increasingly agitated until she brings the scene to an end with the unpardonable insult: "You're a liar!"

The ability to present characters involved in situations almost exclusively through what they say and do—and nearly all Mickiewicz' main protagonists in *Pan Tadeusz* are presented in this way —indicates a creative imagination of a special kind working at the height of its powers. This is an imagination of a visualizing nature, suggesting an artist primarily interested in the external world, less so in the intricacies of his characters' psychological motivations. Other writers with this attitude toward their material include Dickens and Henryk Sienkiewicz.

Mickiewicz' preference for depicting his characters in action is also manifest in the way they are shown preoccupied with the business of the passing moment—arguing, flirting, hunting, eating and drinking, picking mushrooms, or fighting. Yet Mickiewicz can vary his method of bringing a character to life. Sometimes he will let us see one protagonist through the eyes of another (as Tadeusz sees Telimena for the first time, I, 593-610). Elsewhere, he does not hesitate to employ the traditional method of enumerating significant details of a character's appearance, especially of their attire (the count and his followers, II, 107-112).

But the poet's eye is not fixed entirely on his characters. Mickiewicz is a prime example of a Romantic writer in whose work there is often a strong vein of realism. Like Wordsworth, Mickiewicz deliberately cultivated his perception of the outer world, and he was able to convey what his eye and imagination saw in such a way that we are struck by his freshness and accuracy of vision. In *Pan Tadeusz*, his eye is often fixed upon the landscape, observing, for instance, the way poultry behave at dawn: "Already sparrows, hopping about, had begun to chatter in the eaves,/The gander cackled thrice, and after him, like an echo,/Ducks and turkeys shouted in chorus." (II, 354-7) And a rabbit

> Shivering under a stone, pricking up his ears,
> Staring with a red eye into the huntsman's gaze
> And, as if bewitched, aware of his fate,
> Could not turn his eye away, and sat
> Motionless as a rock under a rock.

> (II, 92-6)

Or cattle and birds before a storm:

> A bull paws the earth with his hoof and horn,
> And terrifies the entire herd with his bellowing;
> A cow continually raises her great eye to the heavens,
> Opens her mouth in fright and sighs heavily . . .
> Birds took refuge in the woods, under eaves, deep in grass;
> Only ravens, alighting in droves round a pond,
> Stalk to and fro with ponderous gait,
> Turning their black eyes on the black clouds.

> (X, 27-36)

Almost every page of *Pan Tadeusz* offers examples of the poet remembering what things were like.

There is another sort of realism in the poem that is less immediately apparent but significant in context. This realism occurs as a result of the poet's taking for his material a range of characters, settings, and themes that are representative of a given society at a specific point in time. Mickiewicz' characters are not exceptional or heroic beings, but they are presented as the last (and therefore typical) examples of their society. Instead of a single, outstanding epic hero who governs the action, we are shown a range of typical figures involved in an elaborate network of social relationships. Mickiewicz urges us to regard the judge and his numerous household, the count and his followers, the local gentry, even the Russian garrison as personages characteristic of Lithuania in 1811 and 1812. The lives of all these people converge upon one another, making us aware of the collective nature of this society—the view of society as being a collective is, of course, a feature of realism in literature. The collective is also firmly rooted in its setting, while the proliferation of detail (clothing, food and drink, objects) surrounding the individuals who compose the collective add to the overall feeling of the substantial with which *Pan Tadeusz* is imbued.

The second central theme of the poem—the disparity between appearance and reality—also called for a firm grasp of reality and a measure of objectivity. Mickiewicz develops the theme partly in terms of his characters and expresses his own attitude toward it by irony: Tadeusz' idealization of Telimena in Books I-III brings him to disillusion and self-reproach in Book VIII; the count's peculiar romanticism leads him into taking the goose-girl for the heroine of a romance and into heading the disastrous foray.

But the entire poem is also a statement of Mickiewicz' reflections on the disparity. Writing in 1832 in political exile in Paris, there can have been little hope that Poland, divided and ruled by the three great powers, Prussia, Austria and Russia, would ever again be independent. But the poem gives no indication that the year 1812, when *Pan Tadeusz* ends, was to be one of disaster for Poland. Napoleon's defeat at Moscow meant the end of political hopes for the exiles.

V *Classical Influences*

This brief statement on the realism and objectivity in *Pan Tadeusz* does not by any means exhaust the poem's richness. Mickiewicz' all-encompassing imagination and technical mastery also look back to art of an unmistakably classical kind. The thirteen-syllabic meter with its skillfully designed pattern of rhymed couplets had been a traditional meter in Polish poetry since the sixteenth century and was copiously used during the eighteenth by Krasicki, Naruszewicz and others. Mickiewicz turns this meter into a powerful instrument of expression, with which he can range from passages of imperturbable spaciousness to the hasty give-and-take of agitated speech.

Classical, too, is the way in which Mickiewicz structured the poem on verse paragraphs, each designed as an artistic whole, from which the removal of a single line or couplet would perceptibly damage the poem's form. In the same way, removal of a paragraph would cause irreparable damage. Mickiewicz skillfully uses the varying lengths of his paragraphs as one way of controlling the pace of the narrative and thus avoiding the monotony inherent in a poem of this length (over 9,000 lines). Such control is largely a matter of proportion, which also characterized classical art: the basic narrative structure of *Pan Tadeusz*, provided by action, dialogue, description, summary, and comment, maintains throughout a careful though inconspicuous balance between the component parts. Similarly, Mickiewicz observes the eighteenth-century fondness for careful transitions between the sections of his poem—a fondness the classical writers inherited from the poets of antiquity, especially Ovid and Virgil.

Not, however, that Mickiewicz allowed himself to be bound by these conventions. He chose rather to submit his poetic material to them because they would contribute, if inconspicuously, to the architectonic quality of *Pan Tadeusz*, which owes much to the urbanity and solidity of eighteenth-century poetry at its finest.

VI *The Author's Voice*

Yet the final and abiding impression we gain from a reading of *Pan Tadeusz* as a whole is, paradoxically enough, that of the author's presence. Even though he may temporarily move out of sight to allow his protagonists to act out their scenes, we are nevertheless aware that he will return presently, because he succeeds, at an early point in the poem, in establishing a subtle relationship between his poem, himself as narrator, and us, his readers; and we cannot remain indifferent to the implications of this relationship. Mickiewicz creates it to a large degree through his faultless style, which, because it is perfectly plain and perfectly expressive, cannot be parodied or even imitated. But we cannot, by the nature of things, be concerned here with his style or even diction. However, the relationship is also brought into being by the exploiting of a literary device much used in eighteenth- and early nineteenth-century narrative poetry and fiction: that of making the author's own voice an integral part of the whole work. Mickiewicz brought this device close to perfection: his voice can speak to us in an ironical tone, as when he comments on the count or Telimena; a tone that is serious without being solemn (Jacek's apotheosis in Book X); a satirical tone (on Major Plut); a reflective tone (I, 892-7); or a nostalgic tone in which, however, there is no trace of sentimentality (the final couplet of the poem).[6]

Through this unmistakable voice speaking in varying tones we come to understand the poem's moral, without being subjected to any actual moralizing or statements of moral precepts.

. . . .

Soplicowo and everything it symbolizes constitute a landscape of the poet's imagination, the power of which convinces us of its poetic truth. Critics have discerned inconsistencies in the topography of Soplicowo, but Mickiewicz probably knew and certainly would have approved of Goethe's phrase, *In der Poesie gibt es keine Widersprüche* (1806), ("There is no contradiction in poetry"). The laws governing a work of art are not the laws governing external reality. Inconsistencies that did not trouble the poet need not trouble us. Be that as it may, Mickiewicz' Lithuanian manor house and its occupants have become as much a part of the Polish national mythology as Shakespeare's blasted heath and cliffs of Dover have become of ours.

CHAPTER 7

The Lausanne Lyrics

A HANDFUL of short lyrics, written in Switzerland in 1839 and 1840, marks the end of Mickiewicz' career as a poet. Evidently he had come to feel that lyrical poetry was, in the last resort, the kind of poetry most suited for communicating his innermost feelings and thoughts. The brevity of these poems indicates, too, that the length of a poem has little or no relevance to its significance; what matters is the range of experience we can sense within it.[1]

Mickiewicz' last lyrics are poems of meditation. They begin as a rule with some perception or concrete object upon which the poet builds up to a moment of insight into a general truth. They are epiphanies, or manifestations through the visible world of an invisible life (James Joyce).[2] In Mickiewicz' lyrics, the invisible life is made manifest through a pattern of imagery, because it was in imagery that his creative imagination could assert itself with the greatest freedom.

In one respect, the lyrics can be formally related to the great meditative odes of the eighteenth century, in which a human voice is heard speaking. But there is also a profound difference in tone and feeling in Mickiewicz' lyrics. In the eighteenth-century meditative odes, the voice is not that of an individual. Now, however, we overhear the poet engaged in private discourse with himself, as he contemplates his own life-experience with wonder or sorrow or, ultimately, with acceptance. This is therefore the poetry of human experience: "Over the great clear water/Stood a line of rocks,/And the water's transparent clarity/Reflected their dark faces. . . ." Mickiewicz is meditating on a landscape and describing it in imagery. But instead of the description leading to a speculation on abstract themes, as it generally does in eighteenth-century poetry of this kind, Mickiewicz relates the landscape to his own experience without discussing the feelings or thoughts it evokes within him. The function of the poem is to formulate these emotions: "I see this water all around,/And reflect it truthfully,/And pass by the proud faces of the rocks,/And the lightning-flash. . . ." The theme of the poem, as far as it can be expressed outside the poem itself, is the problem of transience in human life, which Mickiewicz had already considered in the *Crimean Sonnets* more than a decade earlier. This theme recurs in much great poetry, and such poetry often succeeds in a mysterious way in arousing a deeper response within the reader than other poetry of equal technical mastery. The theme, after all, is one which concerns everyone: "The rocks must stand and threaten,/The clouds must bring rain,/The lightning thunder, then be lost,/I—must press onwards, onwards, onwards." Time is seen as drawing everything into itself, and as the poet knows, we can escape it only for a while by pressing forward. Mickiewicz is not expressing mere nostalgia, but a highly complex sorrow: age does not bring rest or fulfillment or even cessation. There is no "easeful Death" to be longed for.

Mickiewicz' artistry in this lyric seems as unstudied, as inevitable as the flow of water. The words he is using do not draw attention to themselves in any way—they are not particularly poetic words, nor are they distinguished from words in everyday use. Apart from being metrical and rhyming, the poem owes little to overtly poetic devices. The spare language, with few epithets (and they are more just than striking) has to carry the total burden of meaning without the artificial respiration of rhetoric. This means that Mickiewicz has mastered the technique of rendering complex feelings with the simplest verbal means. Indeed, the verbal medium is so simple that we almost overlook it on a first reading of the poem. But this simplicity masks sophisticated art, and the words express something that could not be worded otherwise. Mickiewicz is making simple words and simple grammatical structure obey his ideas. The poem's originality lies not so much in the idea as in Mickiewicz' attitude toward it and his way of expressing it.

Although the poem appears to consist of statements, we cannot read it for a prose meaning alone. The last line is not a logical deduction from what has gone before, but the termination of an experience. It is Romantic, even anti-classical, in that we are always in some doubt about the poet's feelings, about what we ought to feel, even about the circumstances giving rise to the feelings. Mickiewicz conveys a persistently challenging sense that the poem has meaning beyond what is stated. The poem is itself part of the total experience it communicates and may even be called the consummation of that experience.

The water, the rocks, the lightning-flash do not constitute an actual landscape, nor are they a random assembly of word-pictures. Their function is not to depict a scene, but to illuminate the poem's meaning. They all point the same way—to this hidden meaning or meanings. At the same time, water, rocks, lightning are the natural language of Mickiewicz' thought; and because they are sufficiently concrete in themselves and are drawn from familiar experience, they render the theme more vividly than any others. They provide the external reality, which, however, is but a surface to be seen through into a greater reality. They are objective images for the inner realm of the poet's psyche. Hence they also have unconscious accretions impossible to state intellectually, and it is these accretions that give them their life, that strike an answering note in an intuitive, introspective reader.

For all the poem's Romantic subjectivity, the poet is taking the trouble to communicate his complex meanings as directly as possible. Unlike such Romantic poets as Shelley or Słowacki, Mickiewicz is not surrendering in this lyric to a hypnotic stream of words, associations, or images that tend to become incantation; nor does he generate ever-increasing imagery until we lose sight of the original thought or feeling which prompted it. This generalization is not intended to denigrate the achievement of the other poets; there is room in the house of poetry for writers with their methods too. But in Mickiewicz' poetry, his critical intelligence is never divorced from feeling and meaning. His poetry evokes not only an emotional, but also an intellectual response.

The poem's surface simplicity, its brevity, its straightforward syntax, the unobtrusive use of repetition—all relate it technically to the ballad. But here the poet is no longer employing these means to tell an anecdote; instead, he is rendering experience that is autobiographical not only to himself but even in some ways to the poem's reader. We receive poetry such as this as an experience

[146]

of our own. The outer world of rocks, water, and lightning is transmuted through the delicate use of technique into an inner world of experience.

Imagery is again at the heart of "Spin love . . ." (1839) and is again used to express a relationship between the outer world of things and the inner world of feelings:

Spin love as a silkworm spins thread from within,
Pour it from your heart as a spring pours water from within,
Uncoil it like gold-leaf that is worked
From a grain of gold, let it flow into the depths, as a spring
Flows underground—rise with it into the air, as the wind rises,
Sow it over the earth, as corn is sown . . .

The meditative character of "Spin love . . ." is enhanced by the final exhortation addressed ambiguously to "you," so that it may refer either to poet or to his reader, or to both: "Thence will come your power, like the power of nature,/And then will your power be like the power of elements. . . ."

In one of the briefest of the Lausanne lyrics, Mickiewicz glances back at his own life:

My tears flowed, pure, profuse,
For my childhood, angelic, idyllic,
For my youth, ambitious, foolish,
For my years of manhood, years of defeat,
My tears flowed, pure, profuse.

This again is the achieved simplicity of a poet who finds his theme too precious for inflation or rhetoric. The simplicity of repetition with significant variation ensures that we cannot miss the main points of contrast. The poem is organized to force a full awareness of its meaning upon us.

Water, that ever-present symbol in Romantic poetry of the poet's innermost mind, recurs in an untitled lyric: "Listen intently to the mute, cold, monotonous sound of water,/And distinguish across the waves the water's thought as through signs. . . ." Similarly, in "A Vision," Mickiewicz gives voice to his continued preoccupation with the workings of his own mind: he suddenly seems to awaken from a terrible dream, and

> The earth and whole world that surrounded me,
> Where earlier there had been only darkness,
> Countless riddles and countless secrets,
> Over which I had often despaired—
> Now I could perceive, as in the depths of water
> When a sun ray falls into its darkness . . .

He is endowed with the power of flight; he becomes the axis of an endless circle, himself motionless, and insight is bestowed upon him—always the desired effect of self-contemplation or analysis. This lyric, like the others, is essentially "modern" poetry, in which the meaning is as important as the feeling and the sound. We are required to ask what the poem means and how that meaning is communicated; there is no "moral," such as eighteenth-century poetry often provides, nor is there a mere surrender to the poem's music.

Although Mickiewicz almost abandoned poetry after *Pan Tadeusz* in 1834, the Lausanne lyrics bear witness to his continued belief that significant emotions must not be lost. Poetry still had the power to register and master experience, however complex it might be. We need not speculate here as to why Mickiewicz published no more poetry, although he lived to 1855. A power had gone, which nothing could restore. All we know is that Mickiewicz reached the height of his creative powers in his middle and late thirties, after which they declined. In this respect he is the epitome of all of us.

.   .   .

The magnitude of Mickiewicz' achievement in Polish literature cannot be overestimated. He revealed a new world to the imaginations of his contemporaries as early as 1819, when he composed the first ballads. He was aware almost from the first that his own special talent as a poet put him far beyond the range of these contemporaries, and he declared: "I differ from the others in that I at once took up a position outside the scope of the old school. In *Romanticism* there is the seed of my future poetry—feeling and faith. I sought and discerned something, like that village girl, and in my later poetry I never strayed very far from that path."

From that time on, each successive work reveals an increase in his poetic range, in his formal and technical mastery, and in the

depths of his experience. The stylistic originality of the love sonnets leads to the inner landscapes of the Crimea, to the powerfully
felt and imagined world of *Forefathers' Eve,* Part III, and to *Pan
Tadeusz,* with its spacious descriptive and narrative power, its
wide understanding of human nature, and its infinitely flexible
verse. These works constitute a body of creative work only a poet
of major stature could have conceived, and they render superfluous any examination of his lesser work—such as *Farys, Ordon's
Redoubt, Three Budrys* and the like—though these would have
made the reputation of a lesser writer.

Mickiewicz shared several assumptions about poetry with other
Romantic writers. These beliefs may be generally stated as follows: first, reality and the outer world surrounding the poet are
proper subjects for poetry; second, the supernatural or supra-
natural, in the form of manifestations of what we may now prefer
to call the unconscious, or psyche, have a profound bearing on
this reality and on human life; and third, the poet's medium of
words is vitally important and must be used with the utmost precision, delicacy, and critical judgement. All three beliefs are
closely related throughout Mickiewicz' work.

Reality meant many things to Mickiewicz, from contemporary
political and social events to the question of the poet's relationship
and ultimate responsibility to society. He knew he possessed a
unique talent and that this talent enabled him to enter realms of
experience from which most of us are barred except through the
medium of a poet's imagination. He also knew, however, that the
possession of this unique talent rendered him in an essential way
responsible to humanity in general and to his own oppressed nation in particular. His duty, his moral obligation—as well as the
possession of his poetic gifts—made him take upon himself the
task of speaking for Poland and, in a way, for any member of
humanity who shared his abhorrence of tyranny and despotism. In
this respect, Mickiewicz stands in clear relationship to the traditions of Renaissance poetry, represented in Poland by Jan Kochanowski and others.

At the same time, Mickiewicz had a strong and interesting personality and was confronted throughout his life with numerous
tensions generated by the reality he had to come to terms with.
These tensions and their solutions give his poetry its universal

reference, as we are offered striking evidence of a human being coming to grips with a complex and often hostile world.

Like Wordsworth, Mickiewicz was always "a man talking to men," with genuine understanding and sympathy. There is no sentimentality in his mature poetry. Feelings were important to him, of course—and he was able to express a considerable range of highly complex feelings—but never did he allow them to swamp his all-pervading sense of reality and the physical environment of life. In Mickiewicz' poetry, feeling is not indulged in for its own sake or to generate disembodied emotion. This does not by any means indicate that he lacks immense potency of suggestion. But even in *Forefathers' Eve*, Part IV, the work in which we come closest to disembodied emotion for its own sake, the outpourings of the distracted Gustav are objectivized into drama and controlled by art.

Reality was part of Mickiewicz' way of thinking, and it provided him with correlatives for his own experience. The detailed accuracy with which the poet's attentive eye observed this reality is, to be sure, an attribute which Mickiewicz possessed along with other Romantic poets. Even the earliest ballad, "This I Love," for all its ghostly anecdote, is firmly attached to reality by the presence of a sceptical narrator, the use of the language of real life, and the localized, specific landscape seen by the poet in perspective—always a sure sign that the writer is visualizing reality as well as imagining it. The presence of society in the love sonnets relates them to contemporary society as Mickiewicz had experienced it. The symbolic landscapes of the Crimea are not disembodied or impalpable but are directly associated with personal events. Here, too, the poet is seen accepting the inevitable transitoriness of life and love with the melancholy resignation of a realist uncontaminated by sentimentality (which loads the writer's material with emotional overtones the material does not warrant).

Similarly, *Forefathers' Eve*, Part III, for all its power of myth, its angels and grotesque demons, sinister dreams, ecstatic visions, and other psychic manifestations, was founded upon Mickiewicz' particular experience in the Wilno prison a decade earlier. He draws upon the real world of Wilno and Warsaw society on the one hand, and upon the world of fantasy on the other. The stage becomes a device for vitalizing and joining the two worlds, and

Mickiewicz' experience is transmuted into poetry by the power of art. In *Pan Tadeusz*, certainly, reality is itself a dominant theme. By identifying with a specific (if imagined) locality, Mickiewicz secures a fuller identification with real life. His understanding of human nature is such that he can tolerate even the silliness of the deluded count and Telimena, though there is implied rebuke in his attitude as well.

Mickiewicz' persistent concern with reality runs parallel to his equally persistent interest in the supernatural. This interest was not a mystical obsession with the occult for its own sake, but a conviction that the supernatural was an integral part of life as we know it. He shared this interest and conviction with many poets and writers of the Romantic age, partly as a reaction against the eighteenth-century mistrust and fear of anything not part of rational experience. In this respect, the Romantics resembled writers of the seventeenth century, when intuition as expressed in mysticism dominated reason and the intellect. In both periods, the universe was intuitively felt to be larger than it was in the classical ages. The absence of psychic life makes much eighteenth-century poetry seem low in tension, one-sided, or even dead for post-Romantic readers.

Mickiewicz examined all kinds of psychic experience, from animal magnetism[3] to the significance of dreams. We may be sure that his critical intellect and his upbringing in the spirit of the Age of Enlightenment informed his inquiries with more than a touch of scepticism, but this is not the point. At first, to be sure, ghosts, vampires, and primitive superstitions offered him picturesque material for ballads and poetic drama. In *Forefathers' Eve*, Part III (1832), however, the function of the supernatural reveals Mickiewicz' more mature conviction that the human personality, or psyche, contains almost indefinite possibilities for good or for evil, if only we can understand how to liberate and set them to work. He realized that the writing of poetry itself, which was the purpose of his life for two decades, depends largely on the ability to liberate these powers, although in his case, as in the case of all great poets, the powers were controlled by the deliberate application of artistic sensitivity and technique.

All poets need to find their own unmistakable voices, but great poets need to find a range of voices by which to express the infinitely greater range of their experience. Naturally enough, as we have seen, Mickiewicz began with a voice belonging to the eighteenth century in his declamatory "Ode to Youth." But he could not be content for long with the stock of words provided by the eighteenth century, and almost simultaneously he discovered a new and original voice for the ballads. The originality of this voice lay partly in its being distinctively regional; but also, and more significantly, this voice proved that Mickiewicz, even at the start of his career as poet, was vastly more sensitive than his contemporaries to the possibilities inherent in his own language. Such sensitivity is an essential attribute in the making of a great writer. Mickiewicz set out with the deliberate and self-conscious (in a good sense) intention of exploiting his native language to the full.

He displays the true creative writer's profound interest and concern with language; and he knew by intuition which words to adopt out of the common fund of vocabulary, which words to abandon as worn-out, and which words to resurrect from past writers. The words he chose to use were precisely the words his poetry—and his less articulate contemporaries—required, if poetry was to be revived from the stagnation of the glossy and hackneyed language prevailing at the end of the eighteenth century. Mickiewicz' words appeal both to the mind and to the senses; they are words that quicken dormant emotions, words that reverberate.

A parallel with Wordsworth again comes to mind here. Like the English poet a few years earlier, Mickiewicz was faced with the task of forcing readers to forget their acquired habits in reading poetry, and of creating a taste by which his own work could be enjoyed.[4] This too is a task facing most great poets, and the fact that Mickiewicz succeeded in accomplishing it is yet another measure of his achievement. Diction was a major problem in solving this task; and Mickiewicz—by his direct, vigorous, subtle, and clear diction—made a specific contribution toward overcoming the generalized, indeterminate quality of his predecessors.

Throughout his career, Mickiewicz subjected inspiration to constant experiment in order to make his poetry an increasingly sensitive instrument, better able to reveal depths and shades of meaning. At one level, the experiments were concerned with problems of diction and versification—technical matters in which we are less interested than poets and critics of the nineteenth century (we prefer to concern ourselves with problems of meaning, symbolism, ambiguity and the like). At another level, the experiments were concerned with the literary genres. Mickiewicz no longer felt obliged, as his predecessors did, to keep the various literary genres strictly apart. So, by way of experiment, he brought to perfection first the ballad, which led to narrative poetry, and finally to the Lausanne lyrics, where he used the ballad technique to express highly personal emotion. In the *Crimean Sonnets,* he experimented with one of the strictest poetic forms known in European poetry, in order to overcome and control the flow of unconscious content.

By the time he came to composing *Forefathers' Eve,* Part III, he was able to reject formal tragedy as practised by the classical writers and to combine myth, spiritual tragedy, and prophetic writing with elements of opera, satire, and even farce (the senator falling out of bed). *Pan Tadeusz,* too, is a blend of literary genres, ranging from the epic and the idyll to what we now call the psychological novel.

At yet another level, the constant experiments reveal Mickiewicz' constant struggle to find the most appropriate means for communicating his private thoughts and feelings to the rest of the world. Through his experiments, he can be watched as he explores the potentialities of human experience more thoroughly than his contemporaries; and through them, too, he learned to contemplate the human situation from a wider range of viewpoints.

But for all his experiments, Mickiewicz also stands firmly within the poetic traditions of his native land. Like Jan Kochanowski in the sixteenth century, Mickiewicz believed in the intrinsic value of poetry, and was not concerned to masquerade as a moralist, philosopher, theologian, or historian—though his poetry could draw upon these matters. He attempted to reaffirm the public role of poetry. This role and the prophetic element seen in his work during the nineteenth century gave rise to a belief that Mickiewicz was "more" than a poet. Like the other major Romantic poets of Poland (Słowacki, Kransiński), Mickiewicz was regarded primarily as a prophetic voice and a bard. Mickiewicz himself helped foster this image, and a mystic cult grew up

around him that came to overshadow his true achievement as
poet. Not until early in our century was he rediscovered in that
light.

The almost impenetrable barrier of language has meant that
Mickiewicz' poetry never extended beyond the frontiers of Poland. This is our loss. Attempts—often admirable in intention—
have been made to render his poetry in a language of wider
familiarity to Western readers. But a poet's native tongue, and
the language he writes in, are one and the same thing. Mickiewicz
and the Polish language—its words, idioms, syntax, associations
—are essentially indivisible. This qualification need not, however,
prevent us from appreciating the magnitude of his achievement.

Notes and References

CHAPTER ONE

1. Gillian Rodger, "A Reason for the Inadequacy of the Romantic *Kunstballade*," *Modern Language Review*, LV (1960), 371-91.
2. Helen Darbishire, *The Poet Wordsworth* (Oxford, 1950), 35-74.
3. A free but successful rendering of this ballad, by W. H. Auden, is published in Clark Mills, ed., *Adam Mickiewicz: Selected Poems* (New York, 1956), 67-69. All the translations given in the present book are mine.

CHAPTER TWO

1. George Steiner, *Tolstoy or Dostoevsky* (New York, 1959), 134-35.
2. Gerhard Adler, *The Living Symbol* (New York, 1961), 299-327, develops the concept more fully.
3. Wacław Kubacki, *Pierwiosnki polskiego romantyzmu* (Harbingers of Polish Romanticism) (Cracow, 1949), 19-60.

CHAPTER THREE

1. Selected sources for the hypothetical "Unconscious" will be found in the bibliography.
2. Leo Spitzer, *Linguistics and Literary History* (New York, 1962), 34.
3. Quoted in *American Imago* XVIII (1961), 54.
4. G. Wilson Knight, *The Starlit Dome* (London, 1941), 99 ff.
5. Joseph Campbell, *The Hero with a Thousand Faces* (New York, 1949; reprinted, 1956), 21 ff.
6. Harold B. Segel, "Mickiewicz and the Arabic *qasidah* in Poland," *American Contributions to the Fifth International Congress of Slavists* (The Hague, 1963), 279-300.
7. Marjorie Hope Nicolson, *Mountain Gloom and Mountain Glory* (Ithaca, 1959), 377.

8. For an illuminating study of the poetry of John Keats in terms of analytical psychology, see Katharine M. Wilson, *The Nightingale and the Hawk* (London, 1964), which appeared after this study was completed.

CHAPTER FOUR

1. Karl Kroeber, *Romantic Narrative Art* (Madison, Wis., 1960) provides an illuminating study of the genre.

2. Wiktor Weintraub, *The Poetry of Adam Mickiewicz* (The Hague, 1954), 131-33.

CHAPTER FIVE

1. Irena Slawiñska, *Sceniczny gest poety* (The Poet's Scenic Gesture) (Cracow, 1960), 91-128, deals with the dialogue in the play.

2. *Times Literary Supplement* (London, August 1964), 758.

3. Carl Jung and C. Kerenyi, *Introduction to a Science of Mythology*, translated by R.F.C. Hull (London, 1950), 66 ff. Also published as *Essays on a Science of Mythology* (New York, 1949).

4. J. Middleton Murry, *Selected Criticism* (London, 1960), 112.

5. Carl Jung, *Archetypes and the Collective Unconscious* being volume IX of the *Collected Edition* (New York, 1959), 143 ff.

6. Harold B. Segel, "Animal Magnetism in Polish Romantic Literature," *Polish Review* VII (1962), 16-40.

7. Jung, *op. cit.*, 219.

8. Campbell, *op. cit.*, 10.

9. Wacław Borowy, "Poet of Transformation," in Manfred Kridl, *Adam Mickiewicz, Poet of Poland; a Symposium* (New York, 1951), 35-56, offers a more traditional view of the process.

10. Mircea Eliade, *Birth and Rebirth* (New York, 1958) examines this topic in detail.

11. Carl Jung, *Civilization in Transition* (Collected Edition, Vol. V) (New York, 1964), 202.

12. A rhymed version is furnished by J. Peterkiewicz and Burns Singer, *Five Centuries of Polish Poetry* (London, 1960), 67-68.

13. Wacław Lednicki, *Pushkin's Bronze Horseman* (University of California Publications: Slavic Studies, Vol. I. Berkeley, 1955) provides the most thorough-going treatment of this topic.

CHAPTER SIX

1. Jerzy Pietrkiewicz, "The Idyll; a Constant Companion of Polish Poets," *Slavonic & E. European Review* XXXIV (1954), 131-55.

2. The line references are to the Polish text.

3. Barbara Hardy, "Food and ceremony in *Great Expectations,*" *Essays in Criticism,* IV (1963), 351.

4. *Ibid.,* 352.

5. For illustrations of this type in Russian plays of the period, see David J. Welsh, *Russian Comedy 1765-1823* (The Hague, forthcoming).

6. Kazimierz Wyka, *Pan Tadeusz* I (Warsaw, 1963), 183 ff.

CHAPTER SEVEN

1. Several of the ideas expressed in this examination of Mickiewicz' lyrical poetry are derived from readings in *Scrutiny* (Cambridge, 1932-1953), too numerous to list here. Professor D. W. Harding, *Experience into Words: Essays on Poetry* (London, 1963) has also helped clarify many points.

2. Richard Ellmann, *James Joyce* (New York, 1959), 87-89.

3. Harold B. Segel, "Animal Magnetism in Polish Romantic Literature," *Polish Review* VII (1962), 16-40.

4. Darbishire, *op. cit., passim.*

Selected Bibliography

Bibliographies in English

Coleman, A. P. and M. M. Coleman. *Adam Mickiewicz in English.*
  Schenectady, N. Y.: Electric City Press, 1940.
Coleman, M. M. *Polish Literature in English Translation.* Cheshire,
  Conn.: Cherry Hill Books, 1963.

BIBLIOGRAPHIES IN POLISH

Semkowicz, Aleksandr. *Bibliografia utworów Adama Mickiewicza.*
  Warsaw: PIW, 1958.
Sliwińska, Irmina, *et al. Adam Mickiewicz: zarys bibliograficzny.*
  Warsaw: PIW, 1957.

PRIMARY SOURCES: *I Collected Works*

Mickiewicz, Adam. *Dzieła.* 16 vols. Warsaw: Czytelnik, 1948-1955.
  The standard edition of Mickiewicz' collected works, including
  letters; has almost no critical apparatus.

II English Translations

Helsztyński, Stanislaw, *ed. Adam Mickiewicz; Selected Poetry and
  Prose.* Warsaw: Polonia, 1955. A reprint of translations by other
  hands, mostly from the 1944 volume edited by G. R. Noyes (see
  below). The *Crimean Sonnets* are included in full and in their
  original order.
Kirkconnell, Watson. *Pan Tadeusz, or The Last Foray in Lithuania.*
  New York: Polish Institute of Arts and Sciences in America, 1962.
  A rendering in pentameter couplets, 12,572 lines in length, as
  compared to the original's 9,843. A number of unfortunate (if
  unavoidable) "translator's words." Professor Harold Segel has
  provided useful notes.
Lindsay, Jack. *Adam Mickiewicz—Poems.* London: Sylvan Press,
  1957. An agreeable, though brief selection, which attempts, in its

small range, to offer a representative survey. Several of the "anthology pieces" not mentioned in the present volume have been included.

Mills, Clark, *ed. Adam Mickiewicz: Selected Poems.* New York: Noonday Press, 1956. Spirited, if very free renderings, by a number of hands, including W. H. Auden. Serious objections against this volume (and the next item, below) by Jerzy Pietrkiewicz should be consulted (*Slavonic and East European Review,* XXXVII, No. 89) (June, 1959), 518-21.

Mills, Clark, *ed. Adam Mickiewicz: New Selected Poems.* New York: Voyages Press, 1957. Complements the previous item.

Noyes, George Rapall. *Pan Tadeusz.* New York: E. P. Dutton, 1917. A pedestrian version, in prose, which may be used in conjunction with Watson Kirkconnell's versified translation, listed above.

Noyes, George Rapall, *ed. Poems by Adam Mickiewicz.* New York: Polish Institute of Arts and Sciences in America, 1944. By far the most copious selection, including *Forefathers' Eve,* Part III, though the versions differ greatly in terms of quality, skill, and taste.

Parish, Jewell, *et al. Konrad Wallenrod, and Other Writings of Adam Mickiewicz.* Berkeley, Cal.: University of California Press, 1925. Includes two of the ballads and the *Books of Pilgrimage,* as well as the complete narrative poem named in the title.

Underwood, Edna. *Sonnets from the Crimea.* San Francisco: P. Elder & Co., 1917. A not entirely successful attempt to keep to the strict sonnet form, which the contributors to the Clark Mills selections (see above) were less concerned to do.

SECONDARY SOURCES: *I. Biographical Studies in English*

Gardner, Monica. *Adam Mickiewicz, the National Poet of Poland.* New York: E. P. Dutton, 1911. Enthusiastic, but long out of date, and sadly inadequate regarding the poetry.

Jastruń, Mieczysław. *Adam Mickiewicz.* Warsaw: Polonia, 1955. A superficial and uncritical account, evidently written "to order" by one of Poland's most interesting contemporary poets.

Pruszyński, Ksawery. *Adam Mickiewicz, the Life Story of the Greatest Polish Poet.* London: Polish Cultural Institute, 1955. An overwritten *vie romancée* of the worst kind.

II. Biographical Studies in Polish

Kleiner, Juliusz. *Mickiewicz.* 2 vols. (the second in two parts). 2nd ed. Lublin: Catholic University, 1948. A monumental work which has superseded all the older biographies. A thorough critical apparatus; contains a number of valuable insights of a somewhat traditional kind; relates the poet's private life to his work.

Pigoń, Stanisław, *ed. Kronika życia i twórczóści Adama Mickiewicza.* Warsaw: PIW, 1957. A minutely detailed record of the poet's life. The first volume covers the period to 1824.

III. Critical Studies in English

Bugelski, B. R. *ed. Mickiewicz and the West.* Buffalo: University of Buffalo, 1956. Five lectures by scholars delivered in 1955 at the Annual Convention of Polish Cultural Clubs; varying in interest.

Kridl, Manfred, *ed. Adam Mickiewicz, Poet of Poland: a Symposium.* New York: Columbia University Press, 1951. The most interesting essay is an English version of the late Professor Borowy's "Poet of Transformation."

Lednicki, Waclaw, *ed. Adam Mickiewicz in World Literature.* Berkeley, Cal.: University of California Press, 1956. Twenty-nine contributors of various nationalities, writing on varying levels of interest.

Lednicki, Waclaw, *ed. Bits of Table Talk on Pushkin, Mickiewicz, Goethe, Turgenev and Sienkiewicz.* The Hague: Mouton, 1956. Two chapters of great interest: on the biographical elements in *Forefathers' Eve,* Part III (111-31), and on Mickiewicz' relations with Pushkin (157-79).

UNESCO. *Adam Mickiewicz 1798-1855: In Commemoration.* Paris: Gallimard, 1955. Yet another symposium, ranging widely in all respects. Professor Weintraub enumerates most of the worst mistakes in his review (*Slavonic and East European Review,* XXXV, No. 84) (1956), 301-3.

Weintraub, Wiktor. *The Poetry of Adam Mickiewicz.* The Hague: Mouton, 1954. While intended as an introduction for English readers, Professor Weintraub had the inestimable advantage of being able to quote the Polish (accompanied by prose versions). His annotated bibliography surveys all the important literature, though Weintraub was naturally unable to include the large amount published in the Centenary Year (1955).

Weintraub, Wiktor. *Literature as Prophecy: Scholarship and Martinist Poetics in Mickiewicz' Parisian Lectures.* The Hague: Mouton, 1959. A searching examination of the poet's Messianic teachings, not dealt with in the present volume.

IV. Critical Studies in Polish

Borowy, Wacław. *O poezji Mickiewicza*. 2 vols. Lublin: Catholic University, 1958. Published posthumously, and based on several university courses. Especially valuable for the bibliographical apparatus.

Dłuska, Maria. *O wersyfikacji Mickiewicza*. Warsaw: PIW, 1955. A brief and schematic survey, with statistics and tables; curiously old-fashioned and inconclusive.

Górski, Konrad, *et al. Słownik języka Adama Mickiewicza*. Wrocław: Ossolineum, 1962. A monumental concordance to all Mickiewicz' writings; still in progress.

Krżyzanowski, Julian, *ed. Ludowość u Mickiewicza*. Warsaw: PIW, 1958. A collection of essays by various hands on the folklore elements in Mickiewicz' poetry.

Krżyzanowski, Julian, *ed. Mickiewicz: siedem odczytów*. Warsaw: Czytelnik, 1956. Seven popular-style lectures, delivered by leading scholars during the Centenary celebrations.

Kubacki, Wacław. *Palmira i Babilon*. Wrocław: Ossolineum, 1951. The eminent scholar declares that a visit to Leningrad gave him a number of fresh insights into Mickiewicz' poetry, especially *Forefathers' Eve*, Part III, which he places against a Russian background.

Kubacki, Wacław. *Pierwiosnki polskiego romantyzmu*. Cracow: Arct, 1949. An erudite, never pedantic study of Mickiewicz' early poetry; refreshingly free from Marxist dogma which was already beginning to gain a hold over literary criticism when the book was published.

Kubacki, Wacław. *Żeglarz i pielgrzym*. Warsaw: Czytelnik, 1954. Deals with the "sailor" motif in Mickiewicz' poetry; the poet's sojourn in Rome; and ends with a stylistic study of the *Books of Pilgrimage*. Marked, like all Professor Kubacki's work, with elegance of style and impressive learning.

Polska Akademia Nauk. *Adam Mickiewicz: 1855-1955*. Wrocław: Ossolineum, 1958. The Proceedings of the International Congress of the Polish Academy of Sciences, commemorating the Centenary, and offering a wide range of international contributions from both West and East Europe.

Przyboś, Julian. *Czytając Mickiewicza*. 2nd ed. Warsaw: PIW, 1956. A collection of essays on aspects of Mickiewicz' poetry by the eminent contemporary Polish poet and critic.

Sinko, Tadeusz. *Mickiewicz i antyk*. Wrocław: Ossolineum, 1957. A monumental, erudite study of Classical antiquity, as reflected in Mickiewicz' work.

Ważyk, Adam. *Mickiewicz i wersyfikacja narodowa.* 2nd ed. Warsaw: Czytelnik, 1954. The author, himself a well-known contemporary poet, relates Mickiewicz' poetic techniques to Polish poetic tradition.

Wyka, Kazimierz. *Pan Tadeusz.* 2 vols. Warsaw: PIW, 1963. Volume I is a study of the poem; Volume II establishes the text. By far the most detailed and rewarding study of the poem, though the late Professor Wyka evidently felt it his duty to recover some well-trodden ground (influence of Walter Scott, the question of the poem's genre).

Zgorzelski, Czesław. *O lirykach Mickiewicza i Słowackiego.* Lublin: Catholic University, 1961. As a one-time member of the Wilno school of "Formalists" (a method of criticism no longer practised in Poland), Professor Zgorzelski's studies adhere very closely, as might be expected, to the "words on the page." The present volume is indebted to his readings of the ballads and sonnets, but Professor Zgorzelski may feel that the views expressed here are a travesty of his own.

Zółkiewski, Stefan. *Spór o Mickiewicza.* Wrocław: Ossolineum, 1952. As the date of publication will show, this work is an orthodox Marxist reading of the poet's life and work.

V. Comparative Readings

This section lists a few items, not directly connected with the poetry of Mickiewicz, which have been of inestimable value in the present study. I gladly admit my debt to readings in *Scrutiny* (Cambridge, 1932-1953), edited by Dr. Leavis.

Abrams M. H. *ed. English Romantic Poets.* New York: Oxford University Press, 1960. A collection of important essays by various hands.

Bays, Gwendolen. *The Orphic Vision: Seer Poets from Novalis to Rimbaud.* Lincoln: University of Nebraska Press, 1964. A penetrating study of imagery and symbols in European Romantic poetry.

Darbishire, Helen. *The Poet Wordsworth.* Oxford: University Press, 1950. A short study, but of especial interest on the *Lyrical Ballads.*

Harding, Denys W. *Experience into Words.* London: Chatto & Windus, 1963. The author is a professor of psychology of the University of London and brings this science to bear on English poetry.

Knight, G. Wilson. *The Starlit Dome.* London: Routledge & Kegan

Paul, 1941. A highly original study of English Romantic poetry by the eminent Shakespearean scholar.

Lednicki, Wacław. *Pushkin's "Bronze Horseman."* Berkeley: University of California, 1955. A richly documented study, fruit of many years research; of special interest to readers of Mickiewicz.

Nicolson, Marjorie Hope. *Mountain Gloom and Mountain Glory.* Ithaca: Cornell University Press, 1959. A thorough survey of landscape poetry, mainly English.

VI. Symbols, Myths, Archetypes

Adler, Gerhard. *The Living Symbol.* New York: Pantheon Books, 1961. Based on clinical material, but ranges widely through myths and symbols, which the author treats from a standpoint of Jungian (analytical) psychology.

Baynes, H. G. *Mythology of the Soul.* London: Routledge & Kegan Paul, 1955. Originally published in 1940, this is an exhaustive study of the symbol and mythical content of dreams and paintings.

Bodkin, Maud. *Archetypal Patterns in Poetry: Psychological Studies of Imagination.* Oxford: University Press, 1963. This pioneer work (1934) is still of absorbing interest to readers of poetry.

Campbell, Joseph. *The Hero with a Thousand Faces.* New York: Meridian Books, 1956. Analytical psychology is used as a key to the inner meaning of ancient myths. First published in 1949.

Campbell, Joseph. *The Masks of God.* New York: Viking Press, 1960. Demonstrates the author's wide knowledge of comparative mythology.

Chase, Richard. *Quest for Myth.* Baton Rouge: Louisiana State University, 1949. A valiant attempt to "rescue" myth from psychology and other disciplines.

Fordham, Frieda. *An Introduction to Jung's Psychology.* London: Pelican Books, 1953. A lucid exposition of some of the main concepts of analytical psychology.

Jacobi, Jolande. *Complex, Archetype, Symbol in the Psychology of Carl Jung.* New York: Pantheon Books, 1959. A more advanced, but not excessively so, study of the three main concepts.

Jung, Carl G. *Archetypes and the Collective Unconscious* (Vol. 9 of the Collected Works). New York: Pantheon Books, 1959. One of the fundamental texts for an understanding of Jung's psychology.

Jung, Carl G., ed. *Man and His Symbols.* New York: Doubleday, 1964. Five introductory essays, intended to popularize Jung's work; beautifully illustrated.

Jung, Carl G. *Symbols of Transformation* (Vol. 5 of the Collected Works). New York: Pantheon Books, 1956. A revised version of one of Jung's most profound and influential works, first titled *The Psychology of the Unconscious.*

Jung, Carl G. and C. Kerenyi. *Essays on a Science of Mythology.* New York: Pantheon Books, 1949. A convincing application of analytical psychology to the Divine Boy and the Maiden archetypes.

Kerenyi, C. *Prometheus: Archetypal Image of Human Existence.* New York: Bollinger Foundation, 1963. A strikingly original, thought-provoking examination of the myth.

Neumann, Erich. *The Origins of the History of Consciousness.* New York: Pantheon Books, 1954. A fundamental, if difficult, contribution to analytical psychology and its application to myth.

Rank, Otto. *The Myth of the Birth of the Hero.* New York: Brunner, 1952. A psychological interpretation of myth by a former colleague of Freud.

Sebeok, Thomas A. ed. *Myth—a Symposium.* Philadelphia: American Folklore Society, 1955. A selection of essays by various hands; not primarily concerned with psychological interpretations.

Wilson, Katharine M. *The Nightingale and the Hawk.* London: Chatto & Windus, 1964. A study in terms of analytical psychology devoted entirely to Keats' *Endymion* and the odes.

Index

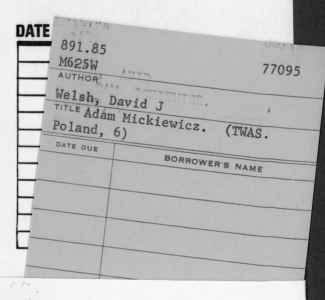